EMBODYING EARTH
Real Magic and Spiritual Self-care
WORKBOOK

SONDRA ANN TURNBULL

GODDESS KINDLED
UNIVERSE

*Healing • Magical Realism •
Experiential Guides • Meditative
Journeys & Soundscapes • Magic*

Copyright © 2019 Sondra Ann Turnbull

All rights reserved. This book or any portion thereof may not be reproduced or used in any manner whatsoever without the express written permission of the publisher except for the use of brief quotations in a book review.

First published in the Netherlands

Original language, English

Editions: 2019, 2021
ISBN 978-94-92724-05-2

Cover design by GKU
Book design and production by GKU
Editing by M.S. Wordsmith, www.mswordsmith.nl
Cover photograph by Jeremy Bishop on Unsplash

This book is not intended as a substitute for the medical advice of physicians. The reader should regularly consult a physician in matters relating to their health and particularly with respect to any symptoms that may require diagnosis or medical attention.

All references and links correct at date of publication

Goddess Kindled Universe (GKU)

www.GoddessKindled.com

For every person who ever pushed my buttons and was a catalyst for growth. I love you and you might never know it. I'm still coming to terms with the fact.

CONTENTS

Table of Experience iii
Acknowledgements ix
Introduction xi

PART I 1
The Still Point 1
Seeing Things as They Are 5
Stories We Tell Ourselves 13
The Balanced View 25
Sacredness of the Ordinary 29
Washing Away 39

PART II 43
Taking the Risk 45
What You Allow 49
Awakening 57
Some Earthy Metaphysics 65

PART III 71
Meeting the Deeper Self 73
Layers 77
Venturing Into Wildish 83
Grounding 95
Tree Talk 101

PART IV 111
Believing in Possibility 113
Too Common to Count 117
Shifting Reality 123
Are You Ready? 131
Resisting Change 143
Finding Balance 159

PART V 165
Courageous Beginnings 167
Ready to Receive 171
The Weight of White 181
Quickening 191
Inviting Curiosity 199
Emotional Shape Changing 207

GOING DEEPER 219
Your Invitation 221
Index of Experience 223
About the Author 225
Books in this Series 227
Our Promise 229

TABLE OF EXPERIENCE

INTRODUCTION
Experience 1 Introduction - Beginning ... xvi
Experience 2 Introduction - First Contemplation ... xvii
Experience 3 Introduction - Plugging In ... xviii
Experience 4 Introduction - Gathering Your Tools ... xxi

PART I CRACKS

Chapter 1 The Still Point
Experience 5 Your Breath - Meditation ... 3
Experience 6 Your Breath - Deepening ... 4

Chapter 2 Seeing Things as They Are
Experience 7 Choosing a Name - Exploring ... 6
Experience 8 Choosing a Name - Trusting ... 7
Experience 9 Choosing a Name - Connecting ... 8
Experience 10 Choosing a Name - Contemplation ... 8
Experience 11 Truth - Contemplation ... 10
Experience 12 Truth - Journalling ... 11
Experience 13 The Sanctuary - Meditation ... 12

Chapter 3 Stories We Tell Ourselves
Experience 14 What is Your Truth - Creating Space ... 14
Experience 15 What is Your Truth - Journalling ... 15
Experience 16 What is Your Truth - Deepening ... 17
Experience 17 What is Your Truth - Contemplation ... 19
Experience 18 Being Seen - Contemplation ... 20
Experience 19 Being Seen - Connecting ... 20
Experience 20 Being Seen - Playing ... 21
Experience 21 Being Seen - Journalling ... 22
Experience 22 Drumming: An Introduction - Mindfulness ... 23
Experience 23 Drumming: An Introduction - Meditation ... 24

Chapter 4 The Balanced View
Experience 24 Intuitive Understanding of Earth - Journalling ... 27
Experience 25 Intuitive Understanding of Earth - Contemplation ... 27

Chapter 5 Sacredness of the Ordinary
Experience 26 Everyday Ritual Moments - Connecting ... 30
Experience 27 Everyday Ritual Moments - Focusing ... 31
Experience 28 Everyday Ritual Moments - Deepening ... 33
Experience 29 Symbolism in Your Surroundings - Connecting ... 34
Experience 30 Symbolism in Your Surroundings - Contemplation ... 35
Experience 31 Symbolism in Your Surroundings - Journalling ... 36
Experience 32 Symbolism in Your Surroundings - Divination ... 37
Experience 33 Grounded Beginnings - Connecting ... 38

Experience 34 Grounded Beginnings - Focusing — 38
Experience 35 Grounded Beginnings - Deepening — 38

Chapter 6 Washing Away
Experience 36 Being Held by the Great Mother - Relaxation — 40
Experience 37 Being Held by the Great Mother - Journalling — 40
Experience 38 Being Held by the Great Mother - Deepening — 41
Experience 39 Being Held by the Great Mother - Meditation — 41
Experience 40 Being Held by the Great Mother - Journalling — 42

PART II DELUGE

Chapter 7 Taking the Risk
Experience 41 Taking the Risk - Breathing — 46
Experience 42 Taking the Risk - Meditation — 46
Experience 43 Taking the Risk - Journalling — 47

Chapter 8 What You Allow
Experience 44 Observing Judgements - Breathing — 50
Experience 45 Observing Judgements - Meditation — 51
Experience 46 Observing Judgements - Lightening — 51
Experience 47 Observing Judgements - Contemplation — 51
Experience 48 Connection to Family - Journalling — 53
Experience 49 Connection to Family - Deepening — 54
Experience 50 Connection to Family - Lightening — 55
Experience 51 Connection to Family - Mindfulness — 56

Chapter 9 Awakening
Experience 52 Your Connection to Self - Journalling — 59
Experience 53 Your Connection to Self - Contemplation — 59
Experience 54 Your Connection to Self - Self-inquiry — 60
Experience 55 Your Connection to Self - Contemplation — 61
Experience 56 As Above, So Below - Contemplation — 62
Experience 57 As Above, So Below - Creation — 63
Experience 58 As Above, So Below - Journalling — 63

Chapter 10 Some Earthy Methaphysics
Experience 59 Unravelling Into the Green - Potion — 66
Experience 60 Unravelling Into the Green - Remedy — 67
Experience 61 Unravelling Into the Green - Invocation — 69

PART III GERMINATE

Chapter 11 Meeting the Deeper Self
Experience 62 The Deeper Self - Contemplation — 74
Experience 63 The Deeper Self - Journalling — 75
Experience 64 The Deeper Self - Playing — 75
Experience 65 The Deeper Self - Deepening — 75
Experience 66 The Deeper Self - Journalling — 76

Chapter 12 Layers

Experience 67 Your Energetic Body - Breathing	79
Experience 68 Your Energetic Body - Breathing Meditation	79
Experience 69 Your Energetic Body - Visualisation	80
Experience 70 Your Energetic Body - Energy Work	81
Experience 71 Your Energetic Body - Energy Work	82

Chapter 13 Venturing Into Wildish

Experience 72 Thin Places - Visualisation	85
Experience 73 Thin Places - Chanting	87
Experience 74 Thin Places - Playing	88
Experience 75 Thin Places - Journalling	89
Experience 76 Listening Through the Thinning - Meditation	92
Experience 77 Listening Through the Thinning - Healing	93
Experience 78 Listening Through the Thinning - Journalling	94

Chapter 14 Grounding

Experience 79 Sensing Earth - Grounding	96
Experience 80 Sensing Earth - Meditation	97
Experience 81 Reconnecting - Visualisation	98
Experience 82 Reconnecting - Deepening	99

Chapter 15 Tree Talk

Experience 83 Leaning In - Listening	103
Experience 84 Leaning In - Embodying	104
Experience 85 Leaning Intimately - Listening	106
Experience 86 Leaning Intimately - Journalling	107
Experience 87 Leaning Intimately - Embodying	108
Experience 88 Leaning Intimately - Journalling	110

PART IV SPROUT

Chapter 16 Believing in Possibility

Experience 89 Believing in Possibility - Contemplation	114
Experience 90 Believing in Possibility - Journalling	115
Experience 91 Believing in Possibility - Playing	116

Chapter 17 Too Common to Count

Experience 92 Invisibility - Moving Meditation	119
Experience 93 Invisibility - Visualisation	120
Experience 94 Invisibility - Shape-shifting	121
Experience 95 Invisibility - Chanting	121

Chapter 18 Shifting Reality

Experience 96 The Possibility of New Direction - Relaxation	125
Experience 97 The Possibility of New Direction - Meditation	126
Experience 98 Balance and Believing - Contemplation	129
Experience 99 Balance and Believing - Embodying	129

Experience 100 Balance and Believing - Playing … 130

Chapter 19 Are You Ready?
Experience 101 Asking for Help - Journalling … 134
Experience 102 Spirals - Moving Meditation … 136
Experience 103 Spirals - Contemplation … 136
Experience 104 Spirals - Journalling … 137
Experience 105 Base Chakra - Contemplation … 138
Experience 106 Base Chakra - Release … 139
Experience 107 Base Chakra - Connecting … 141

Chapter 20 Resisting Change
Experience 108 Fear of Falling - Visualisation … 145
Experience 109 Fear of Falling - Journalling … 147
Experience 110 Fear of Falling - Playing … 149
Experience 111 Change is Exhausting - Visualisation … 151
Experience 112 Change is Exhausting - Deepening … 152
Experience 113 Change is Exhausting - Journalling … 153
Experience 114 Change is Exhausting - Release … 154
Experience 115 God Goddess All That Is - Active Meditation … 156
Experience 116 God Goddess All That Is - Contemplation … 156
Experience 117 God Goddess All That Is - Journalling … 158

Chapter 21 Finding Balance
Experience 118 Fear and Anger - Active Meditation … 162
Experience 119 Fear and Anger - Journalling … 163
Experience 120 Fear and Anger - Deepening … 164

PART V UNFURL

Chapter 22 Courageous Beginnings
Experience 121 The Proportion of Your Courage - Contemplation … 169
Experience 122 The Proportion of Your Courage - Making Magic … 169
Experience 123 The Proportion of Your Courage - Ritual … 170

Chapter 23 Ready to Receive
Experience 124 Seeing Your Life - Journalling … 173
Experience 125 Seeing Your Life - Contemplation … 174
Experience 126 Seeing Your Life - Deepening … 175
Experience 127 The Mucky Stuff - Journalling … 178
Experience 128 The Mucky Stuff - Release … 179
Experience 129 The Mucky Stuff - Cleansing … 179

Chapter 24 The Weight of White
Experience 130 Overwhelm - Sensing … 182
Experience 131 Overwhelm - Deepening … 183
Experience 132 Overwhelm - Journalling … 185
Experience 133 The Safety of the Wild - Journalling … 187

Experience 134 The Safety of the Wild - Ritual	187
Experience 135 The Safety of the Wild - Spellwork	188
Experience 136 The Safety of the Wild - Deepening	189

Chapter 25 Quickening

Experience 137 Outrunning Belligerence - Journalling	193
Experience 138 Outrunning Belligerence - Deepening	195
Experience 139 Protective Instincts - Meditation	196
Experience 140 Protective Instincts - Journalling	197

Chapter 26 Inviting Curiosity

Experience 141 The Past in Your Present - Journalling	201
Experience 142 The Past in Your Present - Visualisation	203
Experience 143 The Past in Your Present - Moving Meditation	204
Experience 144 Questions, Curiosity, and Grace - Playing	206
Experience 145 Questions, Curiosity, and Grace - Playing	206
Experience 146 Questions, Curiosity, and Grace - Playing	206

Chapter 27 Emotional Shape Changing

Experience 147 Your Animal Nature - Connecting	209
Experience 148 Your Animal Nature - Deepening	211
Experience 149 Your Animal Nature - Embodying	213
Experience 150 Shadow Self - Journalling	215
Experience 151 Shadow Self - Moving Meditation	216
Experience 152 Shadow Self - Shape-shifting	217

ACKNOWLEDGEMENTS

Thank yous are more difficult than first anticipated, so I'll stick to the two individuals without whom you would not be holding this book in your hands.

Mariëlle Smith wrangled my errant commas and asked questions that made me swear, made me think, and ultimately helped me create a better book. You are more than an editor.

Hanneke Coolen walked beside me through this whole journey, nudging me back onto the path when I wandered off track and began to burrow into the earth to hide from myself. She is the wise voice that whispers to me shamanic tales of bones and feathers. Her timing is soaked with divine synchronicity.

I love you both, thanks for being in my life.

INTRODUCTION

"Had I not created my whole world, I would certainly have died in other people's."

The above quote, by Anaïs Nin, is the container within which I birthed my magical realism novel, *Affery's Earth*. It is Affery's journey that is reflected in the real magic and ritual of this guide. Each part of *Embodying Earth* begins with a meditation on the quote from the matching part of the novel as focus for your contemplation.

When I was outlining the novel and really gave myself space to sink into this first quote I could no longer determine if I'd been inspired to begin the story because of it, or found my way to the quote because the story I needed to write was so powerful it required its own safe space in which to become manifest.

Each new section of the novel, and this guide, begins with a quote from Anaïs Nin; all the parts of my work weave into the next creative exploration, it's how my mind makes sense of the world, makes sense of me. The quotes gave me a place to return to, to ground and centre. Each was a container in which I could mix the words that would paint the pictures of the next part of my story.

As you work through this guide, your experience might be akin to the cycle of a seed coming to fruit. Such is my intention for you. Read the quote from the top of this section again: "Had I not created my whole world, I would certainly have died in other people's."

Sit with those words. Read the phrases separately, together, slowly; skim and notice words that still your gaze.

Your whole world will crack open and be created anew, it already does that with no help at all from me. Every morning the day is new, every evening the night rakes over the soil of your dreams. Each breath you draw is a world in itself, dissolving into that physical presence you call home; until, all transformed, you blow a different breath away—cast out that which is no longer useful, nourishing.

It is beautiful destruction.

Dying in someone else's world is an everyday occurrence. They are the small deaths of conforming to the other's desire, even though your truth skews off at a different angle. You take the step too far, though you know it will be uncomfortable. It is easy to bury the discomfort, it's invisible—so you think.

Don't worry about the faint tension behind your eyes. The dentist can fix the cracked tooth that you detected with your 3 am tongue. It was the cat clawing over pebbles beneath your bedroom window that woke you, not the sound of grinding molars; and that ache in your jaw has nothing to do with tension. Some simple, over-the-counter worm medicine will kill the crawling squirming, eliminate the instinctive clenching that reaches up through your bowel and into your belly.

Those discomforts are all physical irritations. There's nothing spiritual about them. Spirit is invisible, imaginary. Imaginary isn't real.

What does your world look like? Have you ever considered that question? Is it the same world that you look upon when you rise from your sheets with messy hair to begin again? What you see with the eyes of mundane sight is an edited version of existence, courtesy of your awareness and ego, your protective aspect, your trained and constrained polite manner.

This moment is the dark space that waits to welcome the seed. It is the earth waiting to be damped, poked, sown, and nourished. You will find yourself in the dark, you will glimpse your spirit in the moist magic of a whetted grain of soil that sparkles sharp, ready to aid in the slicing of your outgrown husk.

Why This Book?

In these pages, you will find ways to create your own rituals and make them a normal part of your self-care. You don't need flowing robes, and there are no secret words or symbols. You are the magic and the mystery, and coming to that understanding is the journey.

Do you find yourself whizzing around inside your own head too often for your own peace of mind?

If you want to feel more centred, you will find exercises in mindful focus here. If you want a deeper connection to your core stillness, learning about how to ground yourself is a wonderful place to begin.

With this experiential guide, I offer you ways to explore the world around you and how it connects to the world within, looking through an earth-tinted lens.

This experiential guide is a companion volume to *Affery's Earth*, the first book in my magical realism series, Pull of the Tribe. Each book in this series follows the main character as she journeys to find the place she feels whole, both within herself and within her tribe.

Affery embodies the nature of the earth element. The companion volume you are holding in your hands right now gives guidance for following magical and inner work inspired by her journey. I step you through exercises and practical activities intended to open your awareness to Affery's element.

This is a gradual coming to know yourself.

Take time to wander all the paths I suggest.

Get the most from this experience.

Use this personal workbook to note emotions: dips, or spikes, or even the absence of them. Allow yourself to welcome and spend time with resistance to this exploration as well. At any point in your reading, stop, write down the question or the wondering thought. See where the words take you.

I've created this workbook to partner the originally published experiential guide. It contains the complete guidance, plus provides you with ample space to journal and record your journey. Use it to create your own book of wisdom with your spirit at the heart of the pages.

The joy of dirty feet, finding bits of leaf caught in your hair, and the scent of dark wood awaits. And me, I'll also be waiting in the pages for you.

Why Me?

My background is teaching deep relaxation: the art of allowing, sinking into patience and a state of non-resistance that I call "being soft." If you let me, I can guide you to heal and open to the power of being vulnerable, to discover what are your blockages to healing. To me, healing means becoming more intimate with yourself and the way you flow through your life. Walking the path of a healing journey is allowing yourself to be held while you explore your truths, while you learn to allow (and acknowledge) ways to be congruent with those truths in the person you show to the world.

I know, that sounds terrifying. Stay with me—learning how to hold yourself is part of healing.

Knowing how and when to ask for help is part of holding space for yourself.

I have walked these paths with clients and students since my mid-twenties (in the late 1990s). The main modalities of my practice, then, were guided meditation; reiki healing and, later, teaching; Hawaiian lomi lomi, which I still use to get my energy flowing when I'm feeling particularly stuck—much to the delight of my girlfriend (it is the most delicious full body massage treatment I've ever experienced); and Emotional Freedom Techniques (EFT), also known as "tapping," the full depth and subtlety of which is often underestimated.

I've shared sacred space with people for two decades; writing about my experiences seemed like the next step in my personal healing journey. My understanding of what makes up a healing journey is constantly evolving. I touched on the meaning, above, describing it as a more intimate coming to know yourself. That pulls my concept of healing into the light for closer investigation. Since nobody is broken, ever, what is there to heal from?

We are. Sometimes we understand, mostly we think we understand and that is enough.

Why me? Because I have a way with magic, a way of offering different perspectives and pointing towards hidden paths, a way of leaning with you against the things you find most terrifying and reminding you that you are worth it.

You are worth knowing deeply and understanding more about your own magic and how powerful it is.

Personal Responsibility

You've probably heard the term, victim mentality—it won't have been from me, though. That label conjures a harsh and discriminatory lash designed to punish the person to whom its being stuck. That's a tactic for an in-your-face, ra! ra!, let's go! kind of therapist. I'm a more subtle creature, now. My softening has been part of my own growth.

When I first went into private practise, new clients would often come to their first appointment, discover they were responsible for their own healing and not quite run out the clinic door, but they certainly only appeared in my healing space once. It was confusing for them to even consider they had choices. The idea that they could decide different choices, other than the ones that were making themselves via unhelpful patterning and limiting beliefs, seemed absurd and scary. Learning to create safe space as part of their experience was the way I grew my own experience. Not to mention, it's radically improved my client retention rates.

Let's talk about your responsibility as a client, or in our case with this guide, a seeker.

Until you own your behaviour, thoughts, actions, and emotions will be present in your life as uncontrollable and frightening reflections that bounce at you from every place you look. Unacknowledged (often unwelcome) aspects of your Self are part of what maintains the rigidity, opacity, and distortion of those filters through which you interpret your world.

By stepping into the mucky mire of your least lovely traits, you deepen the strength of your power. The peace that you didn't realise was awaiting your discovery becomes apparent. They are like sticky mud, those traits; they slurp between your toes when you explore them. You will track dark paw prints through your pristine notions; if you are lucky, you won't scrub the prints away immediately or unconsciously.

As you work with my guidance, remember that your own guidance is working right along with you, and neither is more important than the other. Intuition will prickle up the back of your neck, scratch fingernails into your hair to raise shudders of recognition. The exercises I offer encourage you to embrace the things that make you shiver, see with the clarity of closed eyes, stomp in the mud.

Let me show you how to plant a few seeds, how to love the softness of your dark spaces.

Working through some of the following practices with a trusted companion might be something you consider. Especially if you have the intention to work with deeply-held pain. If you expect to descend, are already sitting on the bank of River Styx with this book in your hands, think about calling on someone to be your handmaid, your anchor, your way back to the surface, should the need arise.

Contact a dear friend or a wise aunt, one upon whom you can count to check in with you regularly if they don't hear from you. There is no need to lay your soul bare—unless that is part of your deliberate intention. In fact, you will know you are ready to descend willingly, you will know you have asked the right person to be your handmaid in the act of speaking the words. If it's not time, you won't. And that's okay. Changing your mind is okay, too.

I honour you as you love yourself into wounds and bliss alike.

Introduction to Experiencing

This book is not meant to be consumed non-stop, though you could read the words contained between the covers in a couple of days. If you are anything like me, that's exactly what you'll do: read straight through, then loop back around.

When you read the passages of guided meditation, know that you are in the meditation. Take your time to be completely with the words, in the white spaces between the words. These times are not times to speed-read or skim through. Pause when you want to sink deeper into the journey; close your eyes, even. Then open them to take the next step.

Used as intended, this workbook will be a friend, confidante, instigator, safe space, invitation to something delicious. So plunge into all the dark, moist softness of my words. Burrow in and get buried, then loop back around to your perfect point of experience.

You and your experiences are worth being savoured.

Throughout this workbook you will find plenty of ruled lines to fill with your handwriting and pen strokes. I hope you use all of them, and all the white space, too. You get to decide how you'll fill your personal book of wisdom.

Exercise (1) Beginning

Write out the quote for this section; you'll find it on the first page of the introduction. Use a pen, pencil, crayon, brush—whatever takes your fancy. Read the phrases separately, together, slowly; skim and notice words that still your gaze.

_____

_____

_____

_____

_____

_____

1. How long did it take you to decide what writing implement to use?

_____

_____

_____

2. Have you told yourself that you'll do the practice later and are now preparing to skim the rest of this section before moving on to the next chapter?

_____

_____

_____

3. Did you dive into the activity and doodle, scratch, scrunch paper, break pencil graphite?

_____

_____

_____

Experience 1 Introduction - Beginning

There are no right or wrong answers, only your answers. There is nobody looking over your shoulder, except You. It could be you are so used to turning a blind eye, you won't be looking either. Are you ready to consider the parts of your beauty that are darker and messier than society decrees you have a right to show? If you let me, I'll introduce you to an incredible vista that highlights every painful barb of conformity. Hell, I'll show you how to pluck them from your mind and flick them into the void.

Exercise (II)   First contemplation

What does your world look like? Consider that question. Is the existence you call reality enough? What would you change to make it so?

1. Start by making a list of the things you do every day.

_____

2. Make a mark beside the items on the list that are, for you, the things that feed your spark, your happiness, your sanity.
3. What kind of mark did you make? Is it a heart-shaped doodle, a star, a furry asterisk, a point of colour pushed all the way through the paper?

Experience 2 Introduction - First Contemplation

Exercise (III) Plugging in

Your first grounding lesson: there is more power in this simple action than you have probably ever considered. Take your time, invite all the sensations your body and mind receive to register in your awareness.

1. Go outside and push your fingers into a patch of dirt (if that's not an option, maybe there is an indoor plant whose pot you can visit).

2. Did you skip this exercise, thinking it unimportant? After all, you know what dirt feels like against the skin of your fingers, beneath your fingernails.

3. If you did skip this exercise, get still for a while—yes, right now—and think about why that is.

_____
_____
_____
_____
_____
_____
_____
_____
_____
_____
_____
_____
_____
_____
_____
_____

Experience 3 Introduction - Plugging In

Exercise (IV) Gathering your tools

Before you continue with this book, consider how you feel about writing onto the pages from which you're reading. Are you hesitant to do perform the final act of marking these pages in your own hand? Can you write about your dilemma right here on these lines I've designed for you to do exactly what I'm asking you to do?

_____
_____
_____
_____
_____
_____
_____
_____
_____
_____
_____
_____
_____

Maybe you want to make sure you have a separate notebook and pen. They don't need to be particularly fancy—or maybe they do? Consider the materials you choose. Perhaps you are a journaller from way back and you have empty notebooks all over the house, just waiting for your pen strokes to love their pages.

Journal your experience so far using the following prompts:

1. Do you have permission to embody the magic in this guide?

_____
_____
_____ Continue →

2. The biggest change I want to make in my life is…

3. When I put my fingers in the dirt, the story I told myself was…

Experience 4 Introduction - Gathering Your Tools

PART I

CRACKS

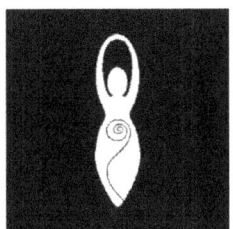

"We don't see things as they are, we see them as we are."
–Anaïs Nin

1

THE STILL POINT

1.1 Breathing Into the Quote

Following is the quote and meditation that frames this part.

> *"We don't see things as they are, we see them as we are." –Anaïs Nin*

This journey is a cycle of growth, as all journeys are. Our starting point is that of a seed: hard, safe, protected inside the non-being of dormancy, sheltered within the all-encompassing potential of its sealed outside layer.

You will always see things around you differently to the person next to you. Everyone sees with eyes veiled by different lives, experiences, languages, lovers, lands. You will comprehend the aspects of reality you are fertile to receive.

Tight packed dirt, parched and cracked, resists a downpour even if the attempted soaking is tumultuous. The effort is just so much noise. Closing your ears to clamour, even if it holds wisdom others perceive as great, isn't a choice—it's simply what happens. Water runs off a hard surface. It won't penetrate until you soften the hidden underworld environment, make it a place from which new growth can emerge. In a case like this, quiet tears are more powerful than stormy pounding.

One small stone, jostled in the storm, dislodges to allow tenderness to trickle in. Long-held beliefs waver with mirage haze and when you are ready to see differently, you do. It happens, and you don't notice the moment of shift. The next breath, the next step, the next blink brings an entirely new world where you continue to see things as you are.

For example, today my pancreas is in distress and I feel nauseated, on the verge of vomiting. I exist in the space between one breath and the next; that is my focus, all I can commit to observing. My perspective is ultra-close-up, every pore in the slope of my nose is clear, I feel the way the minuscule openings in my skin work with my respirative system to strive for balance in my wonky digestive system.

Sometimes I forget about the additional kindness my physical body needs as a human living with acute pancreatitis. That carelessness flows into my emotional body, it strips my ability to care about much at all. The need for deep rest thrusts into the foreground of my view.

My refusal to be kind to myself is the hard-packed earth repelling the softening moisture I need for consistent balance of physical, emotional, spiritual Me. Stubbornness is an earthy trait. Today, I'm closer to bloody-minded than simply steadfast.

Since my last surgery, I no longer feel the excruciating pain of a flare up of pancreatitis; instead, the energy of that overt takeover of my body's pain receptors is disseminated throughout my more invisible systems. I thought the removal of the threat of pain was a good thing, but it took away my easy motivation to be kind to myself. Now, I must be kind because it is the thing that is good for me, not because I'll be carted off to hospital in an ambulance if I don't.

Everything takes on a sick, impossible-to-achieve, unworthy tint when I'm like this. I see the world the way I am, not the way it is. In a few days, I will notice more sparkle, the ease of an idea or action and giggle with delight. I won't notice the moment of shift, it will just be the way I see things after the next blink. Hindsight isn't an instant flash of understanding. Sometimes we must wear our soles to the bone walking a particular trail before even considering the view over our shoulders. We have to trip over that one small dislodged stone many times before tending the deep bruises in those exposed bones.

Experience your breath

Everything is cast in a new light when considered from a shifted perspective.

> A RANDOM NOTE ABOUT MEDITATING IN LOTUS POSITION: There is no need to arrange your limbs in a special posture for any meditation I teach, apart from being comfortable enough to facilitate relaxation. I like the soles of your feet to connect with the floor, but even that is not strictly required.
>
> THIS IS YOUR PRACTICE, MAKE IT YOUR OWN.

1.1 a) **Meditation:** Close your eyes. Take a few breaths, each one slower than the previous, each one pushing deeper into your belly.

Notice the way your body feels when you breathe with this kind of awareness. Feel all the sensations: where your belly resists, the rise and fall of your chest, the knot in your throat, the release in the back of your neck, the way your scalp softens.

Open your eyes and make a note here about what you noticed.

_____
_____
_____
_____
_____

Practise this deliberate focus as often as you want—you'll be breathing even if you don't, so you may as well. You are the meditation.

Experience 5 Your Breath - Meditation

1.1 b) **Deepening:** Make a recurring date with yourself to practise the breathing meditation described above. If the world around you seems to be spinning with no stable thing to hold your anchor, perhaps you will choose several times on the same day rather than different dates. Each time you practise you may notice more of the same sensations, but go deeper into the sense. Perhaps the experience will be something entirely new. Write it all down. Find solace in the patterns. If the patterns seem to be non-existent, don't worry about it, maybe your cycle is longer form.

_____
_____
_____
_____
_____
_____
_____ Continue →

Part I CRACKS

Experience 6 Your Breath - Deepening

2
SEEING THINGS AS THEY ARE

2.1 Choosing a Name

Selecting the name of my novel's main character was a ritual in itself. I wanted her name to symbolise the hidden nature of her personality. One of the delights of being an author of magical realism is designing secrets that await discovery by a reader who is particularly curious: someone like you, who likes to dive deeper than the obvious words on a page, someone who accepts the invitation to take the plunge into the space between those words.

Affery is the first name of the character who embodies the earth element in the novel. Affery means young deer and colour of Earth. Right there, a double layer of hidden magic for my story. So many possibilities! Shape-shifting, elemental power, animal medicine. In shamanic tradition, deer's medicine includes gentleness in word, thought, and touch, and an understanding of what's necessary for survival. She seeks alternative paths to a goal. Bracken is Affery's last name. Bracken is a tall fern with coarse lobed fronds that occurs worldwide and can cover large areas. Another few layers to the magic of her persona were thus added.

During my research of the name I came across a photo of a speckled fawn hiding in a patch of bracken. They were all the elements I have mentioned here in the one picture and I fell in love with Affery in that moment. I grieved, knowing that I would not be able to protect her from the perils and anguish of her healing journey. Not to mention, as the author, I would be the one piling every hurt upon her. But I also had a moment of jubilation, knowing that within her (and therefore within me) resided personal power more immense than she had ever considered could be real.

Part I CRACKS

Experience choosing a name

What name would you choose for yourself? What does it represent about your nature? What does it call you to become?

2.1 a) **Exploring:** Collections of names for nesting parents are scattered across the World Wide Web. Go wild! Try search terms like "names that mean stubborn," "earth goddess names," and "names for hidden secret" to begin with.

_____
_____
_____
_____
_____
_____
_____
_____

Experience 7 Choosing a Name - Exploring

2.1 b) **Trusting:** Go to your bookshelf, close your eyes, run your fingertips over the spines, select the one that wakes to your touch.

What is the author's name?

_____
_____

What are the names of the characters?

_____
_____
_____
_____

Is it a beloved volume that you know word-for-word, or one of those books you always overlook?

_____
_____
_____
_____
_____

Get back on the internet and search for names that convey the flavour of this book.

_____
_____
_____
_____
_____

In this book, what connection to Earth is presented to your imagination? There is always a connection that can be found.

_____
_____
_____
_____
_____

Experience 8 Choosing a Name - Trusting

2.1 c) **Connecting:** Look out your bedroom window, your lounge room window, the window through which you most often daydream. What is the name of the tree that is waving to attract your attention?

_____

What does that name mean?

_____
_____
_____

Experience 9 Choosing a Name - Connecting

2.1 d) **Contemplation:** What is the word that represents the way you feel about this whole activity?

_____

What is the name that holds the essence of that word?

_____

Experience 10 Choosing a Name - Contemplation

2.2 Imp of Truth

Without regard to your horror or jubilation, an imp of truth sits behind your left ear. It rolls its eyes with such intensity you have sometimes heard it. It is like a groaning whisper of breath, and sounds right before you acquiesce to another infringement of your boundaries. It is your reluctance to disempower your Self, your intuition panting with wolfish patience into another moment of being shunted into the background.

The deer and the wolf, they are you: skittish, hidden, knowing, patient—each aspect and animal, nature and instinct in turn.

It doesn't matter how often you beg your imp to hush, be quiet, please—don't make things worse; it will never disappear completely. If you sit quietly, in a space in which you know you will be undisturbed, you will catch your imp in the corner of your mind's eye. Soften your gaze, twitch your head around to the left, hear the wry chuckle of acknowledgment.

There are a number of reasons we ignore the promptings of our imps: laziness, fear, pride, anger, denial—to name a few.

Don't get me wrong, our need to feel safe is an imperative part of preparing our ground to be ready for moistening. "When you are ready to know, the teacher will appear" is not a common saying for nothing. It can be no other way. Forcing matters is not an ideal way to blaze your trail to healing or knowing yourself. All that does is scare the most sheltered parts of your Self deeper into the bracken.

The trick is to gentle those aspects of laziness and fear, pride, anger, and denial into the safe space you have prepared. You must be kind. You must not lie to them; you can't, because they are the library of every instance of past self-delusion.

Experience truth

Telling the truth is at once the easiest and most difficult way we can honour ourselves.

2.2 a)   **Contemplation:** Recall the last instance of your imp of truth making its presence known to you.

Stop right there! That thought—the one you just shoved to the background. That's the one. You know it. Be as kind to the thought as you would be to a shy toddler who smiles tentatively and opens her eyes wide.

Wait. Sit down on the carpet with her. Speak to your thought in words you would use to coax that uncertain little one out from behind the sofa.

Tell her that it's safe, she doesn't have to say anything, you only want to sit with her in silence.

_____
_____
_____
_____
_____
_____
_____
_____
_____
_____ Continue →

Part I CRACKS

___

Experience 11 Truth - Contemplation

2.2 b) **Journalling:** What is the lie you tell yourself most consistently? Take a pen and write this question on the next journalling line. Don't think, start writing!

Write all of the thoughts that are streaming through your mind: The nonsense, the profane, the pleading, the justification—all of it.

___

Chapter 2 — Seeing Things as They Are

Experience 12 Truth - Journalling

2.3 The Sanctuary

Learning to create safe and sacred space for your contemplative work is an important aspect of your magical life. This is the space in which you grant permission, draw boundaries, invite mystery, raise energy, and become centred.

It can feel significant to manifest this safe space in your physical world. Build a nest with soft, cotton-covered cushions; drape the lamps with sheer lengths of crimson organza; drip three drops of cedar essential oil on the wick of a fat, beeswax candle and strike a match to bring it to life. Any, all, none of these actions are necessary to create sacred space.

You are your own sanctuary. It goes where you go. Your sanctuary hovers in between your breaths, slips into the sigh blown over your hot cup of coffee, then melts onto your tongue with the sip that follows. The sacred space of a snot-smeared pillow, shredded by your howl of frustration is as sacred as any vaulted ceiling towards which your most fervent, proper prayers waft.

Experience the sanctuary

The place on the outside is not the place. You are the place; you are the space.

This is the creative spark for what will be a safe, sacred space you visit and revisit throughout your embodying work, and for the rest of your life. The more you sink into this visualisation, the clearer your vision will become. Don't strive for consistency, that will come of its own accord as you come and go. Each time, you'll bring something you need to explore more deeply or put on a shelf and peer at sideways until you're ready to hold it in your hands.

2.3 a) **Meditation:** Close your eyes, right now, wherever you are. Gradually deepen your breathing, feel your way into the lower part of your belly, allow your breath to expand your ribs and lift your shoulders.

When you are ready, imagine a room in the centre of your mind.

Sit with this idea a while. Are you outside the room, looking at a closed door? Are you in the centre of a white-walled space that lacks any feature apart from a large cushion on the floor at your feet? Do you feel welcome? For your first visit, just notice and feel.

Experience 13 The Sanctuary - Meditation

3

STORIES WE TELL OURSELVES

3.1 What is Your Truth?

We all tell a story about who we are. There are several versions of your story: exaggerated, edited, and censored in all the right places for the audience of the moment. Have you ever dared to tell this story to yourself?

No, not that one. Not the portrait you pretend is real: the one that hangs, framed, in the parlour, above the fireplace. Neither is it the one you dragged down the back stairs that night. You took such pains to bash the gilt edges of that secret one against every hard thing you passed; finally, you reached the pit that devours all the ugly parts of your life and hurled it as far as you were able before leaning backwards, so you didn't completely disappear.

I want you to think about that tiny, passport-sized picture that you don't consider important enough to be your whole story. The poppy-seed spec that might blow away forever if you pressed your finger to it and lifted it for closer examination.

Don't worry—I can't see what you are thinking. Go ahead and take a breath. Breathe out. Do that again. Keep doing just that until you are ready to move into the exercises below.

Explore this question of truth even though you don't feel ready to do so. Everything you are is worth expression, it's all You. Truth is what feels right to you in the moment; it is what is real, what's taking place. Truth is a wish that you make with dandelion fuzz; it is also the wonder of watching the fuzz blow away to who knows where, to take root and begin again.

Guess what? The way you undertake this practice now will be different to how you approach it later. Should you (and, I encourage you to, hope you do) come back to these practices at a later date, it will be with the eyes of someone who sees a new world through the filters of other experiences—experiences that you have yet to incorporate into your being.

Experience what is your truth

This exercise is but one of those things that will change you. Remember, there are no right answers, only your answers.

3.1 a) **Creating space:** Take a pen and your workbook, find a place to sit. Are you already making excuses about there being nowhere to sit? Not enough quiet, too much housework to finish off, dinner to make, wine to drink?

When it comes to looking directly at our truth, this part of the exercise, the making space, the allowing, is a practice all by itself.

Experience 14 What is Your Truth - Creating Space

3.1 b) **Journalling:** On the next journalling line write "[Your Name], A True Story." Write the story that comes.

Tell the tale of the thing that happened when you were eight, fell off the swing and broke your arm. Except you weren't swinging on the swing, you were balancing on the top rail of the monkey bars, showing off.

Why did you lie to your mother when she asked you how it had happened?

_____
_____
_____
_____
_____
_____
_____
_____

Chapter 3 — Stories We Tell Ourselves

_____
_____
_____
_____
_____
_____
_____
_____
_____
_____
_____
_____
_____
_____
_____
_____
_____
_____
_____

Experience 15 What is Your Truth - Journalling

3.1 c) **Deepening:** On the next journalling line write "[Your Name], A True Story." Skip ahead in your life a few years and write the next story that comes.

_____
_____
_____
_____
_____
_____
_____ Continue →

Part I CRACKS

Do this a few times.

Chapter 3 — Stories We Tell Ourselves

Can you see a pattern?

Experience 16 What is Your Truth - Deepening

3.1 d) **Contemplation:** Write a story called "Writing True Stories" to explore your experience of this practice. Are the stories you have been writing truth, or only based on a true story?

Chapter 3 Stories We Tell Ourselves

_____
_____
_____
_____
_____
_____
_____

Experience 17 What is Your Truth - Contemplation

Have you just skipped over that whole section of practice, telling yourself that you are not a writer, don't like to write things down, can't spell well enough (even though you are the only one who will see the results)? You are a storyteller whether you know it or not. I know this about you, because you are human and we are built to tell and hear story.

Forget about writing it down, if that is what's holding you back. Pick up your smart phone, open your laptop, open an app on your tablet, get as techie as you like. Now press record on your voice memo, video recorder, capture mechanism of choice, and tell the story!

I'll repeat this until you hear it: there is no wrong or right way to do any of the practices I am guiding you through, just YOUR way.

3.2 Being Seen

Somehow, looking at the bigger picture often means we lose sight of ourselves, our part in the pattern, the knotty tangle in the tapestry. That's the point, isn't it? To pull back far enough that the tangle transforms into a delightful quirk of design.

You are an entire frieze of Big Bang to dead universe plastered on the walls of a circular life. It's time to plant yourself at the centre and spin with delight rather than fear.

It's okay—take a breath. One step, one twirl at a time.

Experience being seen

There is very little you do that, when looked at from the proper perspective, is not meaningful and entirely magical. Let me try that again: everything you do is magical, whether you look at it from a particular angle or shut your eyes. Yes, you are that powerful.

3.2 a) **Contemplation:** Tell me, what is the reflection you most assiduously ignore when you walk by it? Did you realise it was important before I asked the previous question?

When you catch this shunned reflection in the edge of your gaze, which part do you allow yourself to see?

I challenge you to look. Next time you pass, I want you to look on purpose. Remember to breathe when you do.

_____
_____
_____
_____

Experience 18 Being Seen - Contemplation

3.2 b) **Connecting:** Get a small mirror. Is it a compact or more like the broken shard of an old mirror? Is it plain or decorated around the edge?

Be deliberate about your observations, take the time to consider the subtle layers of meaning you are seeing. How does your mirror selection reflect the subtle layers of you? Are you able to soften, to allow the bigger picture into your awareness?

When you are ready, gaze into your own eyes. Blink slowly and gaze on. Breathe into your belly—I'm reminding you because chances are you were holding your breath. What do you see?

_____
_____
_____
_____

Experience 19 Being Seen - Connecting

Chapter 3 — Stories We Tell Ourselves

3.2 c) **Playing:** For this exercise, you don't need a glass mirror; in fact, any reflective surface that is NOT a conventional, modern mirror is what I want you to find. The mirror you choose will form part of the magic of the experience.

Is your reflection distorted? What colour shines through as a tint over your whole form? Can you see only a vaguely human-shaped smudge?

Play!

_____
_____
_____
_____

Experience 20 Being Seen - Playing

3.2 d) **Journalling:** Write it all down: feelings, insights, fears, frustrations, amusement. Let this be merely the first instance you take the time to play with your reflection; you are opening the door to powerful personal connection.

_____
_____
_____
_____
_____
_____
_____
_____
_____ Continue →

Part I CRACKS

Experience 21 Being Seen - Journalling

3.3 Drumming: an Introduction

A powerful way to clear sight is through the beat of a drum, the thrum of bass through your chest, the zing of a soaring note that pins your shoulders back. There, it opens a moment of clarity that stuns you with physical sensation; then the rhythm changes, and you drop back into your shoes.

Drumming is a skill that has been with you since before birth. You formed the counter beat to your mother's rhythm as you grew in her womb. Each thump of your heel against her rib, a muffled bass note, the staccato ripple of hiccoughs that triggered her to shift in position as she slept.

You embodied the instrument, were the drum. You are the beat.

Experience drumming: an introduction

This is an exercise in mindfulness. Your job is to be still and open your awareness to how you feel, what you see, where you resist.

3.3 a) **Mindfulness:** Take yourself for a walk. Yes, I know I said your job was to be still—it is possible to be still while walking. Trust me; stillness is a state of mind. It's the way you approach the activity, approach yourself. There is constant motion in stillness.

As you walk, what beat do you notice? Is it the thud of your shoes against the pavement? Is it the irregular whoosh of cars speeding past? Is it the bump of your bag against your hip? Is it a mess of colliding noise with no discernible rhythm? It's going to be a different experience every time. Notice.

_____
_____
_____
_____
_____
_____
_____
_____

Experience 22 Drumming: An Introduction - Mindfulness

3.3 b) **Meditation:** Lean back in your chair. Place your right hand over the upper portion of your left breast until you feel like you are cupping your heartbeat in the palm of your hand. Feel the rhythm of your life.

That's all. Stay here until you are done.

What are the thoughts that streamed through your mind? What were the ones over which you lingered? Did your breathing quicken, or slow? How long were you able to hold your heart?

_____
_____
_____
_____
_____
_____
_____
_____
_____
_____
_____
_____
_____
_____
_____
_____
_____
_____

Experience 23 Drumming: An Introduction - Meditation

4
THE BALANCED VIEW

4.1 Intuitive Understanding of Earth

Earth is never apart from the other elements. The aspect of magic to which I assign the label of earth contains all the other elements within it. Understanding the way the elements flow together, frame, impede, carry, amplify each other is part of the healing way of embodying this elemental magical practice. This feeding into and out of elements underpins many ancient, or traditional, healing philosophies. Seeking balance inside the flow is an instinctual part of being human.

In attempting to segregate the elements, you would miss the wonder of a balanced view. When the presence of one element overshadows the others, pushes them to the sides and thrusts itself to stand centre stage, there is imbalance.

Much in this tiny blue world of ours that is overburdened, or overindulged seems to create a superfluity of one element over the others. It is an attempt to force human will upon an eternal universe. The Goddess is all about balance; she will only indulge egoic machinations for as long as it entertains Her. Attempting to protect yourself from aspects of an element you perceive as dangerous because they feel overwhelming is the only danger. There is nothing to fear in acceding to the flow. However, dam it up and you are destined for something spectacular and painful—either from the blockage as it festers, or the explosion when She finally releases it. The Goddess doesn't tend to ask for permission first.

I'm always striving for balance. Even though this book is a guide to exploring the earth element in magical ritual and I'm continuously pulling the narrative to that focus, you are actually working with all the elements as they relate to earth in all the exercises (I just don't draw your attention to the fact). You may find working with particular elements more challenging than others, and that's completely normal. We each have our own affinities, strengths, aptitudes and natural abilities, that's why some elements might feel dangerous.

Discovering which element is your intimate connection is thrilling, it feels like music tuned to your personal key. As you come to know the other elements, your magical work becomes a chord sounding to your soul. We are at the very beginning of your exploration; water, air, and fire are books still in my future. I hope they are also in yours.

Experience intuitive understanding of earth

Before I further pollinate your mind with my opinions, it's time to explore your own.

4.1 a) **Journalling:** Do some intuitive digging into your instinctive understanding of the element of earth; you may unearth a forgotten treasure. What are the things you do, ways of being, of moving through the world that suggest it is an "earthy" influenced happening?

For example, the way you always trail your fingers over the trees beside the path, or collect random leaves and pebbles, finding them in the pockets of jackets years later. These elemental tokens have no purpose, they just feel lovely in your hand, seem to respond to your touch. Perhaps that is the purpose.

_____
_____
_____
_____
_____
_____
_____
_____
_____
_____
_____

Chapter 4 The Balanced View

_____
_____
_____
_____
_____

Experience 24 Intuitive Understanding of Earth - Journalling

4.1 b) **Contemplation:** How difficult is it for you to connect with the earth element? Are you a natural tree-hugging, barefooted wanderer?

Are you curious, but shy to open up to what feels base and dirty?

Remember, these questions are intended to spark new ways of thinking, a shifted perspective, a few extra blinks prior to what might have been an automatic answer.

_____
_____
_____
_____
_____
_____
_____
_____
_____
_____
_____
_____

Experience 25 Intuitive Understanding of Earth - Contemplation

5

SACREDNESS OF THE ORDINARY

5.1 Everyday Ritual Moments

The presence of ritual in our lives is another way we hold ourselves in sacred space. You might think that creating sacred space is essential prior to ritual. I suggest that the awareness of any act, thought, moment, makes what you are noticing sacred. Your notice casts a net of impervious power over the space; your intention makes it sacred. I would go further and declare that it already was. There is no more innate holiness in a book of sacred text than there is in the way milk swirls into your coffee as you stir galaxies into the dark liquid.

Ritual can take place entirely in the imagination. Visualisation is a powerful tool for improving the execution of an action. Since this book is about embodying Earth, though, let's get sensual for the next exercise.

Experience everyday ritual moments

Think about the phrase "earthly plane of existence." Approach this section of practice from that state of mind. You are an earthly being, a spark of Divine manifest in the body you take to the toilet every day, the skin that you take for granted, the clumsy misstep that you curse, the nimble fingers with which you tie your child's shoelace. All of these things can be objects of ritual, or acts of ritual, if you are awake to the opportunity.

> **5.1 a)** **Connecting:** Make a list of things you do every day. There is nothing special about these acts; you perform each series of movements automatically. It could be the way you pack your bag for work in the morning, prepare your travel mug of tea and sip it on your way to the

bus, hang the washing, walk the dog, wipe your bum, kiss your lover's cheek in greeting.

___

Experience 26 Everyday Ritual Moments - Connecting

5.1 b) **Focusing:** Select one of the things on your list from 5.1 a) and write out the series of unconscious movements and decisions that go into its performance. Giving these acts attention is the beginning of creating ritual magic.

___

Chapter 5 🝮 Sacredness of the Ordinary

_____
_____
_____
_____
_____
_____
_____
_____

Experience 27 Everyday Ritual Moments - Focusing

5.1 c) **Deepening:** For the next week, make your selected item your daily ritual. You are the only person who will know there is any difference to what you are doing—the extra-gentle touch of fingertips, a softer and longer inhalation of the scent, pouring your entire attention into the moment through your sight.

The only shift is in your mind. Your hands and body will move in the same ways. This will be your secret.

I'll let you in on something; magic is ordinary acts performed with intention and mindful focus. That's it. That's all? I know, it's not as easy as it sounds, that's why it's called magic.

Day 1 _____

_____
_____
_____
_____
_____
_____
_____

Part I CRACKS

Day 2 _____

_____
_____
_____
_____
_____
_____
_____

Day 3 _____

_____
_____
_____
_____
_____
_____
_____
_____

Day 4 _____

_____
_____
_____
_____
_____
_____
_____
_____
_____

Chapter 5 Sacredness of the Ordinary

Day 5 _____

_____
_____
_____
_____
_____
_____
_____

Day 6 _____

_____
_____
_____
_____
_____
_____
_____

Day 7 _____

_____
_____
_____
_____
_____
_____
_____

Experience 28 Everyday Ritual Moments - Deepening

5.2 Symbolism in Your Surroundings

There is something in the flash of lightning, the ticking of leaves blowing against the window pane, the rumble of thunder that vibrates up through the seat of your chair. Each is a voice that speaks to the moment. Auguring the meaning is natural. What is the knowing inside the catch of breath that makes you blink as your awareness merges with the sudden intrusion of the symbol? That's how quickly instinctual magic surges up and dissipates.

Interpreting archetypal behaviour and the art of symbology are built into your existence. The pull in your gut that tells you not to take the next step is an example of that instinctual wisdom.

The instinct to trust yourself is moulded into your bones. You move through the world with the strength of ages infusing the framework of your form. Listen to its whispers, the constant tug, nudge, prompting, surge of clarity. Every moment, you are the filter between the world and your awareness of the world. It could be that your filter is clogged and needs a good power wash, or bang to loosen the dust.

Your awareness of the world is an entirely internal matter. Everything you experience is filtered through your physical form, your senses. The depth of your understanding and ability to interpret why this weirdly shaped stone beside the path, or the title of that book you picked up in the library by mistake are important symbols is subjective. The exercises in this guide are a good way to begin to clean your filter. Imagine how building a consistent embodying practise would awaken you!

Spiritual self-care: maintenance for the human filter since the beginning of time.

Experience symbolism in your surroundings

Look out the window, or better still, go outside and find a place to sit on the ground for this activity. Take your notebook with you—make it a habit to do so; you think you will remember the insight that strikes you, but you probably won't. Magic can be elusive, that's part of the delight.

5.2 a) **Connecting:** Tune into your surroundings. Use all your senses. Maybe you detect the scent of dry earth, damp in the distance from approaching rain; feel the scratch of grass in the palm of your hand as you prop yourself up, unused as you are to sitting on the ground; in the edge of your gaze, catch the tumble of leaves as they chase each other around the base of the tree beneath whose shade you rest. The leaves chuckle with dry voices as they play.

Experience 29 Symbolism in Your Surroundings - Connecting

Chapter 5 — Sacredness of the Ordinary

5.2 b) **Contemplation:** What season is it? How does that affect the way you feel? Have you ever considered the way your body flows with the changes in season: the cycle of potential, surging growth, falling away, rest?

Experience 30 Symbolism in Your Surroundings - Contemplation

5.2 c) **Journalling:** Let yourself imagine that each of the things you notice with your sensual self has a voice and is speaking to you, telling you stories and whispering advice. Write it all down, no matter how fanciful your doubting mind is trying to make you believe you are.

Part I 𝒫 CRACKS

Experience 31 Symbolism in Your Surroundings - Journalling

5.2 d) **Divination:** Write a question on the next journalling line. Listen for the answer.

_____
_____
_____
_____
_____
_____
_____
_____
_____
_____
_____
_____
_____
_____
_____
_____
_____

Experience 32 Symbolism in Your Surroundings - Divination

5.3 GROUNDED BEGINNINGS

Have you experienced the impossibility of anchoring in the face of that which would sweep you away, an oncoming force that feels unstoppable?

Grounding can be as simple as a good stomping to wake the sensation in the soles of your feet, separated from the earth almost constantly by shoes and floors and towers that scrape the sky. When was the last time you walked with bare feet on bare earth? Is that too dirty for you? Would you need to wash or brush the dirt away as soon as possible? Yes? (Imagine me smiling with delight here.) Wait until we get to the muddy parts!

Experience grounded beginnings

Whenever you feel off-centre, disturbed, disconnected, try some of this practice to bring calm and balance to your stance.

5.3 a) **Connecting:** Stand up. It seems obvious: simple grounding, standing with your feet on the floor. But are you really standing? Feel. Let your senses soak through the soles of your feet, the soles of your shoes, connect with the surface that you are standing upon. Balance on all the corners of your feet. Feel the support of your body and the way gravity holds you.

Experience 33 Grounded Beginnings - Connecting

5.3 b) **Focusing:** Now, unclench you backside. Yeah, I know—feels good! You didn't know how tightly you were gripped there, did you? Repeat 5.3 a) with a relaxed butt. Energy starts to flow more freely, through more of your body and not just your legs.

You can do this same exercise when sitting. Try it now. Remember to feel your feet the next time you are in a meeting, or want to float away from the situation in which you find yourself.

Experience 34 Grounded Beginnings - Focusing

5.3 c) **Deepening:** Perhaps you are practised at grounding and already use these or similar techniques to feel connected. You are a whole body (and more, but now's not the time to go into that) capable of touch.

Press your palm to the ground, the arm of the chair, the table, and feel as you were feeling with your feet.

When lying down, do you get turned around inside your visualisation when attempting to feel your feet on the ground? Your skin is the largest sensory organ your physical body has, and your whole back is covered with the stuff. Feel into the ground with the whole of your body, whichever part of it is facing in the downward direction.

Experience 35 Grounded Beginnings - Deepening

6
WASHING AWAY

6.1 Being Held By the Great Mother

Great Mother, Earth Mother, Gaia, Great Goddess are some of the anthropomorphic labels we place on our concept of earth embodied. If I could gaze upon you from the pages of this book, I would whisper your name and remind you that all of those images swirl inside the brilliance of your eyes.

Those powerful Mothers stride with your steps. She wills you to dive into the undergrowth of Her hidden places, slide along the slippery banks of Her creative channels. She catches you at the edge of the crevice, nudges you over the edge, comforts your hurts at the bottom of the pit.

None of these great creative ideals is outside of who you are.

From when we are young, we are taught to be alert to the possibility of danger. Trust is earned only to be shaken, which teaches us to be wary of the world. Our misplaced trust proves that we must even be alert to ourselves. By picking up this book you began learning how to trust anew. Through embodying the magic held by these pages, you are learning to hold yourself, to know yourself. Keep going; sink deeply into those wounded places, there is healing inside your magic.

Experience being held by the Great Mother

Don't worry, I'll get you there by degrees, I promise not to drag you straight to the bottom of the deepest chasm of your pain. I trust you to go as far as it's time for you to go. Just read the final two paragraphs in "Personal responsibility" in the introduction again.

Part I CRACKS

6.1 a) **Relaxation:** Find an armchair that supports your back, maybe the corner of your sofa will suit, or stack some pillows against the head of your bed—something like that. I want your physical senses to remind you that you are safe and held. Now, sit into your nest.

That's it.

Are you able to do just that? Sit with yourself?

Experience 36 Being Held by the Great Mother - Relaxation

6.1 b) **Journalling:** Journal your experience. How long were you comfortable? Did you begin to remember other more important things that needed to be done almost immediately?

_____

Experience 37 Being Held by the Great Mother - Journalling

Chapter 6 Washing Away

6.1 c) **Deepening:** Build on the previous relaxation practice. Sit into your nest, close your eyes, focus on your breath. Each exhalation allows you to sink back into the safety and comfort of your space, yourself, and ultimately into the greater Self where you lose your edges and simply are.

Take the time to do all the steps in this section. Repeat each step if you like, spread the whole thing out over hours, or days—whatever you need.

Sitting and breathing sounds simple, perhaps it sounds pointless; it's anything but either of those things.

_____
_____
_____
_____
_____
_____
_____

Experience 38 Being Held by the Great Mother - Deepening

6.1 d) **Meditation:** Bring a light cover with you this time. A blanket, shawl, sarong, length of fabric, something that will suit your climate and mood. Line your nest with the cover. Repeat step 6.1 c) and (when you know it is time) pull the cover around your shoulders, maybe even over the top of your head.

Imagine it is the cloak of the Great Mother and she holds you in her lap. She cradles you in the most profound safety and softness you have ever experienced.

Experience 39 Being Held by the Great Mother - Meditation

6.1 e) **Journalling:** Was being held by the Great Mother easier than sitting with yourself in 6.1 a)? Journal your experience.

_____
_____ Continue →

Part I • CRACKS

Experience 40 Being Held by the Great Mother - Journalling

PART II

DELUGE

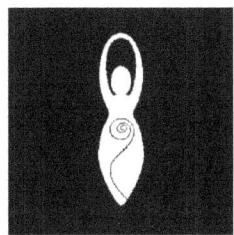

"And the day came when the risk to remain tight in a bud was more painful than the risk it took to blossom."
—Anaïs Nin

7
TAKING THE RISK

๏

7.1 Breathing Into the Quote

Following is the quote and meditation that frames this part.

"And the day came when the risk to remain tight in a bud was more painful than the risk it took to blossom." –Anaïs Nin

The next step in our cycle of growth takes us closer to the destruction that feels impossible. At the beginning, change always feels like the hardest thing to do—especially when movement forward, or in any direction for that matter, feels sure to signal the end. Beginnings are just endings from a different point of view.

The last chapter gave you some tools to crack the hard shell you've spent years polishing, applying hardener to, plastering over any chinks that appeared. In this chapter, we are going to feel into the crack, pull it wider, flood it with attention.

When faced with the potential you hold in your being, it's scary. What if you open that door? What happens to life as you know it? The person you might be afterwards will be entirely different, perfectly whole, and the same person you always were.

I know, that sounds like a snake eating its tail. You're correct. Think about it for a while. Have you ever considered that you are already whole, unbroken, perfect? What feels broken is not wrong; what feels worn out, including all the patches and frayed places, is perfect.

It's okay to feel uncertain, and if you want to take a pause I understand. I've taken many pauses in my journey. Pausing to consider is part of the way, not an obstruction to it. Your timing is your own and you are the expert of you.

Remember though, I've got you; my privilege is not only to offer these words for you to read, but to hold you through this awakening as you surrender to the depth of your own wisdom.

Experience taking the risk

Become acquainted with your resistance to change. I'll help you learn how to be curious and extend the tips of your fingers to feel the crack in your shell, how to explore your uncertainty and love it, using your breath to focus.

7.1 a)   **Breathing:** Close your eyes. Take a few breaths, each one slower than the previous, each one pushing deeper into your belly. Notice the way your body feels when you breathe with this kind of awareness.

Feel all the sensations: where your belly resists, the rise and fall of your chest, the knot in your throat, the release in the back of your neck, the way your scalp softens.

Experience 41 Taking the Risk - Breathing

7.1 b)   **Meditation:** Locate a place where you feel resistance to your breath. It will be somewhere that stays tight and controlled.

Keep breathing into your belly; allow your body to move with the flow of in and out while you feel around.

It might take a few times sitting in this practice to achieve what you consider a result, but every time you do this—staying curious, remaining gentle in your exploration—you become more intimate with the cracks. You are learning to trust yourself.

Experience 42 Taking the Risk - Meditation

7.1 c)   **Journalling:** Journal your experience. Did you locate a crack only to feel it disappear the instant you noticed it?

_____

_____

_____

_____

Chapter 7 Taking the Risk

_____
_____
_____
_____
_____
_____
_____

After you've sat in this practice a couple of times, do you notice the same points of resistance appear and vanish? Do they take longer to vanish each time? Do they feel softer each time? Does your breath avoid the resistance entirely, flowing around it like a stream swirling in eddies around rocks and weeds?

_____
_____
_____
_____
_____
_____
_____
_____
_____
_____
_____
_____
_____
_____

Experience 43 Taking the Risk - Journalling

8

WHAT YOU ALLOW

8.1 Observing Judgements

There is a certain sensation that rises when you are on the verge of sleep. It feels like your spirit is slipping its bonds and escaping your physical form. What if I told you that you are not separate parts at all?

You might be used to thinking in this separated way without even knowing it's what you are doing. It's a very human way of thinking. We categorise and label life all the time—it makes us feel safe. I want to encourage you to observe rather than fixate. Consider how relaxing it is to not have to know for sure about something before you allow it to exist.

Let me break that notion down a bit.

The universe exists. It is. You are part of that is-ness. There is not You + Universe, existing as separate parts. Bring it in closer if that idea is too huge. What do you picture in your mind's eye when you think about Nature? Were you included in the picture, or were you looking at landscape and animals in the wilderness, a television-style nature documentary?

We like to separate human creation from natural creation as though they are opposite forces, one pushing the other out of balance or striving to recapture it, often with a deity or two sitting in overwatch. Again, this is a very human way of making sense of a universe that exists regardless of our understanding. Approval is not required—how terrifying.

All of the labels we use to impose an entirely imaginary control upon a chaotic existence are judgements. What is allowed, what is dangerous, what is worthless, what is important are some familiar ones.

Have you noticed how painful it is when you attempt to halt a cycle? I say "Attempt," because a cycle is never really stalled. We exist in a state of whole and constant motion. Pain is what results from resisting what is. It's confusing, like looking into a mirror and seeing something unexpected reflected back at you. In this way we conjure our own personal versions of motion sickness. Dis-ease, imbalance, and distress manifest in our bodies and minds when we attempt to halt cycles.

Here's a slice of kaleidoscopic pattern for you: your attempts to stay the flow and the resulting pain are parts of the cycle, too. This thing you call living? You can't do it wrong.

Experience observing judgements

This is an exercise in self-inquiry. I encourage you to open up to the following steps, allow me to hold you while you deliberately practise kindness with yourself. Together, we've got this, lovely one.

8.1 a) **Breathing:** Settle into a comfortable chair, breathe into your belly—easy breathing meditation—nothing to do except to focus on the way your breath moves in and out of your body.

Soften it further than that, nothing to do except notice.

Just notice your breath.

Experience 44 Observing Judgements - Breathing

8.1 b) **Meditation:** Think about your day so far; chances are you've done more than slip from your bed to this chair. Which action did you sidestep today? You will recognise the pattern of behaviour I'm talking about if you use the following phrase as a prompt. "If I take this action, [something specific] will happen as a result, and I don't want to feel the way that result will make me feel."

For example, "If I tell him what I think, he'll mock me in front of the whole meeting, and I'll feel stupid."

Pinpoint the moment, the decision that caused you to swerve and redirect your action around an event you predicted was destined to carry you closer to a discomfort.

What is the answer that surges forward in your awareness? Maybe it was more of a twitch than a surge?

_____
_____
_____
_____

Experience 45 Observing Judgements - Meditation

8.1 c) **Lightening:** Settle back into noticing your breath, knowing that, as you do, you're safe. Yes, it's true, you're safe and I'm not trying to trick you.

Consider how much time you spend telling yourself imaginary tales. The discomfort you identified in the previous exercise, the one you took such pains to avoid, was not guaranteed to eventuate, and anyway, this is memory—time travel fiction. Allow your breath to calm and slow.

Experience 46 Observing Judgements - Lightening

8.1 d) **Contemplation:** Go back into the answer you received when I asked which action you sidestepped. If you didn't recognise an answer, repeat the meditation in 8.1 b) and transition to 8.1 c) to lighten and breathe when you feel the need to regroup.

Try to stay with the answer, allow it to be—without trying to polish any tarnish away. For whom are you trying to make your thoughts pretty? Whose judgement are you preparing to receive?

_____
_____
_____
_____
_____

Experience 47 Observing Judgements - Contemplation

8.2 Your Connection to Family

We are conditioned from birth to consider giving way to our immediate family as something vital. I still hear my mother's voice echo in the back of my mind, "Don't rock the boat," when I'm feeling the stirrings of belligerence within the context of sibling or paternal interaction. I've spent so long believing something dreadful would happen if I let my point of view into the world, I now have difficulty allowing myself to relax with my own thoughts. It's one of the reasons there are so many contemplation exercises in this book.

We must accede to the will of family for the greater good of the whole unit. Another time I'll delve into group dynamics and personal motivations of individual family members for maintaining the illusion of a cohesive unit. That discussion includes things like personal safety and an externally fuelled sense of security. But for now, I'm moving you into the concept of group-think. What does that actually mean? This is behaviour that can trample personal feelings of unique expression beneath the hoofs of the herd.

Family is the group we are connected with, the tribe to which we are tied, the blood that binds us to a particular lineage. Family is also the relationships we choose: lover, spouse, adopted child, bosom friend. Are not all humans of the same ultimate family? Let that sink in, it's a vast concept.

While we are all of the one energy, we are unique expressions of it. It's okay to own that. It's okay to step into that personal sense of self on our way to a larger understanding of universal Self.

What is your understanding of this one energy concept?

Take a moment to think about what it means to you. Explore how you feel this connection today. Not how you remember it yesterday, last week, seven years ago when so-and-so lorded their awakening to a highly elevated spiritual awareness over you. (What an arse!)

Experience connection to family

Here are some prompts for you to work with in your exploration.

8.2 a) **Journalling:** There was a moment today when you felt connected to something, some awareness larger than what you consider to be the edges of yourself. It may not have been a particularly powerful sensation. You might have to sit with this point of self-inquiry to invite clarity.

Get still and just write nonsense for a while to let it come forward in your mind. There is wonderful strength in nonsense. It teaches us patience.

Chapter 8 What You Allow

That universal Self can peek through at unexpected moments, an appearance so subtle it's easy to miss. That deep sigh as you voided your bowel, the release and surrender to an action that, let's face it, works best when unhindered. Just write your nonsense until it makes sense to you. Be curious.

_____
_____
_____
_____
_____
_____
_____
_____
_____
_____
_____
_____
_____
_____
_____
_____
_____
_____
_____
_____
_____
_____
_____
_____
_____
_____

Experience 48 Connection to Family - Journalling

8.2 b) **Deepening:** Before you commence this step, please remember that you are safe and have permission to take as much time as you need. This is not a race to enlightenment, this is loving, personal contemplation. Ready? Okay.

Look at that moment of connection you just wrote about in 8.2 a), but this time through the filter of your general family opinion—as though your family was looking at your writing, seeing your thoughts.

What sensation does that create in your gut? Breathe. Stay with it. Skim over the surface first if that's what you need to do. You don't have to plug your nose and cannon ball into the centre right away.

You can come back and peel layers as many times as you like.

_____
_____
_____
_____
_____
_____
_____
_____
_____
_____
_____
_____
_____
_____
_____
_____
_____
_____

Experience 49 Connection to Family - Deepening

8.2 c) **Lightening:** Get some coloured pens. Write your name near the centre of this blank space. Write the names of family members as close to your name as you feel close in connection to them. Draw lines between you and them in the colours and patterns that represent each connection.

Experience 50 Connection to Family - Lightening

8.2 d) **Mindfulness:** Whose names did you feel compelled to place closer to your own than you initially wanted?

_____
_____
_____

Take that question for a walk. Yes, I mean literally—get up, put your shoes on, and walk out the door.

Picture that closer-than-desired name where you left it. Imagine you are holding the line that you drew to connect it to your own name. Now, walk. How long will you maintain your grasp on the line? How quickly will you walk to distance yourself? Will you walk in a straight line, or around the block to loop back on it, tie it in knots? Will you turn it into a game and play jump rope with it?

_____
_____
_____
_____
_____
_____
_____
_____
_____
_____
_____

Experience 51 Connection to Family - Mindfulness

9

AWAKENING

9.1 Your Connection to Self

We all want a wise friend whose advice is consistently good, something to be trusted.

You probably have someone to whom that description applies in your life. They popped into your mind when you read the phrase "wise friend" in the first sentence of this section.

Trusting yourself enough to seek your own advice is something that you may never have considered an eligible course of action. But you will have heard the phrase "higher self." You'll have some kind of sensation, an image of what your higher self is.

When you relax into soft space, become captured by the texture of a flower petal in a sunny garden, wander through an autumn-coloured forest, watch leaves shimmer in the breath of a constant breeze, you meet that higher self. It's the connected part of you. The part of you that is All. It's when you forget your edges and simply are, without space, outside of time.

Humans have the need to categorise and label. We want to understand and this is part of how we construct a framework upon which to hang our lives. We make connections between what we consider uncontrollable and the nearer, more intimate movements of living our lives, and, in this way, imagine that we have satisfied that elusive craving to manage and control. But while the cravings persist (and they will, so long as we attempt to capture the unexplainable in a box), we are never truly sated.

Part II DELUGE

Experience your connection to self

I'm going to ask you to grab a pen and your notebook and do some journalling again. The act of getting the words and thoughts out of your head and making them real on the page is powerful. Writing opens an off-ramp from the insane looping and wondering that some questions trigger.

Use one point at a time as the focus of your journalling. Allow words to flow without censoring yourself. Use detail in your descriptions; let that be a way to sink into the moments you're writing about.

9.1 a)   **Journalling:** Who is the person who became your wise friend, the adviser of the way to live your life? Write a biography, an introduction to reacquaint yourself with everything you remember about them.

_____
_____
_____
_____
_____
_____
_____
_____
_____
_____
_____
_____
_____
_____
_____
_____
_____
_____
_____

Chapter 9 Awakening

_____

_____

_____

_____

_____

_____

_____

Stop.

Go back to the exercise described above. I encourage you to take some time with it before reading further. This is part of learning how to hold space for yourself. Trust that the next words I've written will still be on this page when you come back to them.

Experience 52 Your Connection to Self - Journalling

Did you give yourself the gift I offered? You are worth this time, Sweetheart. Let your eyes float back to 9.1 a) and receive it.

9.1 b) **Contemplation:** How much of the biography from 9.1 a) did you embellish? Go through your journal entry and highlight each instance of polished truth, note each glanced-over reality.

Experience 53 Your Connection to Self - Contemplation

9.1 c) **Self-inquiry:** Select a specific instance of censorship contained in the biography and write about why you needed to make it a pretty word picture rather than a real portrait.

_____

_____

_____

_____

_____ Continue →

Part II))) DELUGE

_____
_____
_____
_____
_____
_____
_____
_____
_____

If the thought of pulling the moment microscopically close feels undoable, observe the journal entry as a whole and soften into your motivations for sanitising the piece. Yours are the only eyes on this work. It's okay to let yourself in, sweet soul.

It's time to breathe. Remember to give yourself space between the practices in this book. This is not a race; it's a winding (or unwinding) path through the labyrinth of your innermost space.

Experience 54 Your Connection to Self - Self-inquiry

9.1 d) **Contemplation:** Give in to the story you are writing. And you are telling a story, whether you knew it the moment you opened this book, or are beginning to see it now. Let go of the need to control, to understand, and simply flow into the adventure. There is only one difference to any normal day of making your way through the world. In this book, I'm inviting you to include yourself as part of the story as well as being the observer, as well as being the author.

You have the universe inside you and it longs to know itself. So stop taking yourself so seriously!

What does this invitation to tell your story mean to you? In what way do my words call you to give in, open a way, soften to your process? Can you feel the parts of you, the different characters? Writer, reader, subject of the tale, universal connection observing with eternal knowing.

___

Experience 55 Your Connection to Self - Contemplation

9.2 As Above, So Below

As with every esoteric concept, there are many ways to consider the phrase "as above, so below." Your interpretation will be filtered through your life experience. In fact, each time you consider the concept, it will take on new colour, be shifted by your new perspective.

Part II 𖡼 DELUGE

"No man ever steps in the same river twice, for it's not the same river and he's not the same man." -Heraclitus

The impermanence of your infinitely expanding universe is the river that you can never step into twice. If I wanted to really get into your mind and stir things up, at this point I would tell you that you can't step into it anyway—because you are the universe and it is you. There is no into or out of. You are one never-ending, glorious mess of star stuff.

When I'm paying attention, there are times I feel like I am the cauldron into which the universe pours Her essence, the mixing pot where ephemeral possibility mingles with the grit and beauteous darkness of earth. I'm the space that accepts it all and churns it into a purely human experience of wonder.

Experience As Above, So Below

This experience calls for some craft supplies. Pull out the brushes and paint, coloured pencils, crayons, pastels. Hell, grab the glue from your child's school supplies and get messy with glitter and torn up magazine pages. Scissors? Find those, too.

9.2 a) **Contemplation:** What is your personal interpretation of "as above, so below"? What picture does it conjure up and plunge you into? Where does it transport your senses? Take some time to centre yourself in this image before you let loose with bringing it to life on the page.

Experience 56 As Above, So Below - Contemplation

9.2 b) **Creation:** Get the largest sheet of paper you can find. Sticky tape some A4 pages together to create a larger canvas. What comes next is all you. Collage creation is chaotic and freeing if you let it take you beyond the borders of what is allowed.

There are no rules for this exercise. Spill your interpretation of "as above, so below" onto your canvas.

Experience 57 As Above, So Below - Creation

9.2 c) **Journalling:** Journal your experience. Was it easy, difficult, mad, glorious? Did it take you hours to place the first carefully trimmed picture in just the right spot on the page? Are your fingernails still stained with the paint that you slapped and swirled with your palms over the blankness of the page? Did you decide it was too silly and skip over the experience entirely?

No rules can be the most challenging rule of all

_____
_____
_____
_____
_____
_____
_____
_____
_____
_____
_____
_____
_____
_____

Experience 58 As Above, So Below - Journalling

10

SOME EARTHY METAPHYSICS

10.1 Unravelling Into the Green

You possess a body that grants you wonderful abilities. You have some combination of being able to see, smell, taste, touch, and hear. Each of us holds a unique mixture of these senses and they are truly wonderful, inviting you to connect to your life and world in tangible ways. They aren't the only ways to experience your life and world though.

The spectrum of light and colour stretches far beyond the capabilities of our human eyesight. You believe it exists because scientists have equipment that can prove it is there.

What about when they can't?

There was always a time when things that we now take for granted couldn't be physically experienced, or measured, or proven. There always will be.

Metaphysics delves into the stuff of an experience or thing that goes beyond the physical and expands into the unknowable realm of spirit. This is where curiosity beckons to the scientist who wonders what more there is: the one with an adventurous heart and mind—enough to answer the call. The scientist probably won't allow that it could be a spiritual call, however.

I do.

Metaphysics is the basis of energy medicine. Things such as vibrational essences, blessings of the sacrament, homeopathy, spiritual healing and practice, prayer, meditation, acupuncture, lomi lomi, essential oils are all ways to experience a wider sense of healing and well-being.

I've experienced the same sense of awe and wonder in church watching a waterfall of energy suffuse the priest as he prayed over the wafers and wine as I have walking the edge of an autumn-tossed cornfield with its bare earth and rows of remains. Each is medicine; all is medicine—if you choose to see it that way.

Experience unravelling into the green

Do you remember making potions when you were a child? Mixing dirt, flower petals, berries, water in the backyard, knowing it wasn't complete and holding your dish up to the air to add some of the wind that tangled your hair? Tipping Mum's special toner down the sink in the bathroom and using the bottle to mix a multicoloured concoction of shampoo, conditioner, and soap while you sat in the cooling water of a bath that seemed to last an eternity? You're going to do it again—it's time to mix some potions and call in some magic.

Though by no means an exhaustive use of the ingredients mentioned here, this is a good place to begin.

10.1 a) **Potion:** Warm fragrance filling your nostrils, mingling with the tang or sweetness over your tongue, soothing your throat and heart and belly as you sip. The experience itself lends depth to any moment if you take the time to notice. Here are a couple of extra dimensions to add to the existing magic of having a cuppa.

Experience 59 Unravelling Into the Green - Potion

All blends described here are my own, the benefits explained are the reason I use the particular ingredient. You are the expert of your body and your experience may be different from mine, so pay attention to your intuition and what your body feeds back to you if you choose to try any of the following.

Chamomile Calm

Grounded and earthy taste, with hints of apple and floral sweetness.

A tea infusion made with chamomile flowers is beneficial for your nervous system, great for emotional healing, calming anxiety, and triggering relaxation. This potion is a digestive tonic, supporting liver function, and can help settle an upset stomach or irritable bowel.

For women, it is a mild remedy for irregular menstruation triggered by tension or stress and alleviates premenstrual pain by relaxing aching, tense muscles.

Chapter 10 ~ Some Earthy Metaphysics

Chamomile may increase the effect of sedative substances (benzodiazepines and anxiolytics) and has an additive effect with coumarin anticoagulants (warfarin).

Wild Raspberry Woman

Distinctly herbal flavour, try adding honey.

Raspberry leaf infusions have been used for centuries by women for its supportive benefits during pregnancy, but are beneficial to women at all stages of life for a healthy reproductive system.

This tea, which strengthens the uterus and pelvic muscles, can ease PMS symptoms and endometriosis.

Additionally, use the potion as a mouthwash, swishing to help alleviate gingivitis or gum disease symptoms.

Drinking raspberry leaf tea may not be a wise choice for those who've had unusual pregnancies or delivery experiences.

Possible contraindications for people taking anti-anxiety or sleeping medications.

10.1 b) **Remedy:** Two essential oils that that I'm surprised every home doesn't have in the medicine cabinet are lavender and tea tree. I use them all the time—such intrinsic elements in my daily rituals that they are simply another entry on my regular shopping list, like soap.

Experience 60 Unravelling Into the Green - Remedy

Soothed Scrapes

Use tea tree essential oil directly on the skin to treat cuts and scrapes, bumps and itches. It has powerful anti-bacterial, anti-fungal, antiviral, and antiseptic properties. A drop on a cotton bud applied to a cold sore that has not yet erupted can halt it in its tracks, or reduce the time it takes to heal at the very least. This is one use I can loudly vouch for!

Tea tree has a strong herbaceous and woody scent. It eases mental stress and purifies the mind and body of emotional wounds, even as it purifies the skin as described above.

Inhale the scent to feel more calm and self-sufficient, to smooth mood swings, sooth panic attacks and anxiety. Use it to stimulate clear thinking and release old emotional wounds.

Lullaby

Lavender essential oil is another that you can apply directly to your skin to soothe and cleanse bites and grazes; it's also good for healing bruises. It has a sweet, floral, soothing aroma.

Dab a drop at your pulse points and temples, the base of your skull to relieve headaches and soften into a compassionate space of sleep.

Use lavender when you don't know what else to do. It promotes rest and brings on a gentle sense of well-being, helps to soothe deep sadness, and conjures feelings of balance.

This ancient remedy, all by itself, is a quiet power-pack of relaxation.

One day you will take your understandings, sensations, intuitions, and inner knowings and create your own ways of calling magic into your life. Here is an example of how to play, how to embody your practice.

10.1 c)   **Invocation:** Chanting and dancing have long been ways to raise energy and create sacred space. Don't panic, I'm not going to ask you to do either. Yet.

Channelling elemental magic into your tea infusion and remedial potion for additional depth and purpose can be an entirely silent affair, internal, intimate. Focus your attention, know that what you intend is done.

Calling in the element of Earth

At the moment of midnight:

Take your potion or remedy in your hands. Cup it, cradle it, treat it as the most precious artefact.

Stand, facing north, balanced on all the corners of your feet. Feel into the ground with your soles.

In simple language, using your own words, ask for the patience and wisdom of Earth to answer your call, mingle with the awareness you've gained by burrowing down through the soles of your feet.

When you feel a tingle, see the images of blended energy in your mind, just know it is so, breathe in. Pull the element of Earth back up into your body, be the channel, feel it flow up through your feet, legs, torso—down your arms, through your palms, and into your potion or remedy.

It is done.

Experience 61 Unravelling Into the Green - Invocation

*If you want more information or are at all concerned about how these potions and remedies might affect you specifically, talk it over with your local naturopath, healer, or trusted health care provider.

PART III

GERMINATE

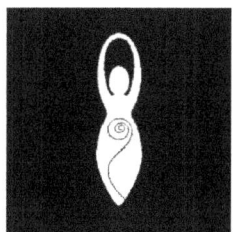

"Each friend represents a world in us, a world possibly not born until they arrive, and it is only by this meeting that a new world is born."
—*Anaïs Nin*

11

MEETING THE DEEPER SELF

11.1 Breathing Into the Quote

Following is the quote and meditation that frames this part.

> *"Each friend represents a world in us, a world possibly not born until they arrive, and it is only by this meeting that a new world is born."* –Anaïs Nin

In the moments after destruction, there is a sudden intake of breath. We taste the debris created from breaking through our hard outer shell. Our exposed slice of tender green belly is grimy with the dark earth in which we've been buried.

You can't go back though. Remember to consider this cycle as that of a seed. The cycle flows, once conditions are right and your insides bulge with the need to be released, to grow, to be something more, your husk will split.

It must.

Keep breathing. This is where you feel the edges of new existence and recognise that it's wonder on the other side of hesitation and fear, not oblivion. You don't have to knock on the door to seek entry into this new world; you have already passed over the threshold. Every moment births another new world within you, and each vibrates with the knowledge that you have arrived. You are cracking open your eyelids, peeking. Keep breathing.

Meeting your deeper self is quite an undertaking but you don't always have to wait for an invitation; you are allowed to go seeking answers, truths, awareness, memory.

Part III GERMINATE

Experience the deeper self

It might feel as though you are out of control, which you are, but so is everything and everyone around you. Perhaps you've arrived at this point not of your own volition but after being forced, pushed, nagged, dragged. Is that true? Are you resisting to the last? Let go. Let go and let's get you feeling around into the darker corners of this new space you are carving out for yourself.

11.1 a) **Contemplation:** Read the quote at the top of this chapter. Spend time with the words, the spaces between the words. Notice when the little voice in your head urges you to go and make a cup of tea, reminds you there are dishes to wash, flat out tells you that you have no friends.

Notice, and then read the quote again. Notice, and know that I am here with you.

Experience 62 The Deeper Self - Contemplation

11.1 b) **Journalling:** Take your journal and write about what has come up for you. What does this quote mean to you? Never mind anything else I've said in this chapter so far—what does this quote mean to you?

_____
_____
_____
_____
_____
_____
_____
_____
_____
_____
_____
_____
_____

Chapter 11 Meeting the Deeper Self

_____
_____
_____
_____
_____

Experience 63 The Deeper Self - Journalling

11.1 c)   **Playing:** Get some card stock and your other crafty bits and pieces: glue, scissors, stuff to stick on, cut up, rip. Maybe you have some watercolour or calligraphy pens tucked into a drawer that you always meant to use, but as you lacked the necessary artistic expertise, they are still unopened. It's time to crack that shell, darling.

         Make an invitation to invite yourself into the world of your deeper Self.

         Serve notice that you are planning to visit.

         Record the words here.

_____
_____
_____
_____
_____
_____
_____

Experience 64 The Deeper Self - Playing

11.1 d)   **Deepening:** Where do you need to take your invitation now? Where is the delivery point? Do you have to tuck it into the hollow of the tree in your backyard? Will you bury it deep beside your favourite path in the forest? Will you put it in the back of the drawer that held the forgotten art supplies?

Experience 65 The Deeper Self - Deepening

11.1 e) **Journalling:** Where did this invitation experience take you? Did you end up where you expected? Was it easier than you thought it would be? Are you feeling joyful at the prospect of your invitation being accepted or dreading the response?

_____
_____
_____
_____
_____
_____
_____
_____
_____
_____
_____
_____
_____
_____
_____
_____
_____
_____
_____
_____
_____
_____
_____

Experience 66 The Deeper Self - Journalling

12
LAYERS

12.1 Your Energetic Body

There are many ways to study your body's energy system. You will have heard about ancient traditions, or, more probably, modern interpretations of ancient traditions. Aboriginal and native medicine ways include the emotional and energetic bodies as a matter of course. Teachings based on the chakra system might feel new age but the knowledge dates back to between 1,500–500BC India. Reiki is a personal spiritual practice that, in western-based energy medicine, is known almost exclusively as a hands-on healing method, but its threads weave back into Japanese Zen Buddhism.

After thirty years of experience and study, I've come to the conclusion that the true core, original motivation, and awakened practice of all established religions and spiritual philosophies have more in common than not—from High Priestess to Pope.

When beginning to consider the energetic aspect of your body, it can be quite a shift in thinking. If your physical body is the manifested result of multiple layers of energy that connect to larger energetic patterns, which are all streams flowing through an ever-expanding universe—that's an opening of awareness that might prove too large to grok in one go.

It's as simple and complex as this: everything is energy in motion. And everything—every thing—is connected.

You already sense energy instinctively. When you walk into a room and know without seeing anyone's face that there has been an argument—the air seethes with warning and your energetic body picks up on that. Sometimes, it is so palpable, goosebumps prickle up your arms or a blush swells up your cheeks.

Part III ᛜ GERMINATE

Experience your energetic body

The most obvious physical manifestation of energy moving through your being is your breath. This is where we will begin. I know, there's a lot of breathing in this guide—that's how precious and powerful it is, this thing you do, take for granted every day whether awake or asleep. Imagine the works of wonder you might achieve by simply giving it attention, acknowledging the abundance of your own life force, the quiet tenacity awaiting your call.

I've listed two breathing exercises consecutively below. If you don't have much experience with breathing meditation, please take the time you need to work through this section. Leave generous space (hours or even a day) between sessions and take the time to practise the first exercise 12.1 a) few times before moving on to the next one. You are learning how to hold space for yourself.

12.1 a) **Breathing:** Bring your attention to your breath. Allow it to remain relaxed and smooth, just notice its movement, its flow in and out of your body.

It may naturally deepen into your belly, move your attention with your breath on an inhalation and flow down from your chest into your belly until the lowest parts of your belly are rising and falling as you breathe.

At the end of each exhalation, pull your belly in to expel the tail of breath and pause. At the fullness of each inhalation, take one more sip of breath and pause.

When you feel it is time, allow your breathing to relax into its natural rhythm.

Deep breathing is elegant magic and raises your energy, strengthens flagging determination, reinforces will, and engages inspiration.

The first time you do this exercise, you may only feel comfortable to continue for under a minute. Each time you engage with your breath this way, you will be able to sustain the practice a little longer.

After each session, record how you are feeling and how long your practice lasted. Notice how you feel. Lighter? Larger? Clearer?

_____

_____

Chapter 12 ꩜ Layers

_____
_____
_____
_____
_____
_____
_____
_____

Experience 67 Your Energetic Body - Breathing

12.1 b) **Breathing meditation:** Take time to settle into a comfortable seat, with your feet flat on the floor. Feel around into your body, down into the corners of your feet. Feel how your soles connect with the floor, anchoring you.

Imagine a tiny golden spark deep in the centre of your body, between your navel and spine. Each time you inhale it pulses a gentle glow.

Allow your breathing to remain relaxed and cycling through its natural pattern of in and out. Simply allow the tiny spark to respond to your breath.

The glow that is generated by the spark builds up in your body, gradually filling your whole torso, flowing into your arms and legs, neck and head, feet and hands, hair and ears, fingers and toes.

Stay with it, witness the constant magic of your breath, and bask in the wonder of its glow.

Experience 68 Your Energetic Body - Breathing Meditation

12.1 c) **Visualisation:** Sit comfortably, straighten your posture: head over heart, heart over pelvis, rest your hands wherever they are comfortable.

Bring your attention to your crown point, your seventh chakra. Imagine a flower bud resting there on top of your head. It is vital, alive, waiting.

Now imagine a soft stream of light flowing towards the flower bud from somewhere far away.

Visualise the flower bud opening its petals to the light raining down, welcoming the light into its centre.

See the light flowing through the centre of the flower and branching out into a web of glowing roots that gradually fill your entire body, all the way to your fingers and toes.

The glowing roots push down through the soles of your feet and into the earth beneath. You are the conduit that brings heaven into Earth.

You can do this standing or sitting—try both ways at different times and consider the way energy flows through your body.

_____
_____
_____
_____
_____
_____
_____
_____

Experience 69 Your Energetic Body - Visualisation

Let's use the symbology of flower buds opening for the following exercise, too. The final two exercises in this section will benefit from flowing out of your state of being at the end of 12.1 c). I encourage you to experiment by doing exercises 12.1 c), d), and e) together as a complete practice, then separately at other times.

12.1 d) **Energy work:** Turn your palms upward. If you are sitting, raise your arms slightly so your hands are not resting against anything. Look at your hands, allow your fingers to curve naturally. It looks like you are holding invisible balls, doesn't it? Visualise a flower bud in the centre of each palm, protected inside the gentle curve of your fingers, resting inside the

Chapter 12 — Layers

bottom of the invisible balls you are holding. Imagine the buds slowly opening.

As the petals open, a soft glow emanates from the hearts of the blooms. The flowers continue to open until their petals rest against the inner slope of the invisible balls and the glow fills the balls.

You are holding orbs of glowing energy. What does it feel like? What colour is the energy? Weigh the energy by bouncing your hands gently. Does the energy have weight?

_____

_____

_____

_____

_____

_____

_____

Experience 70 Your Energetic Body - Energy Work

12.1 e) **Energy work:** Generate balls of energy in the palms of your hands, as you did in 12.1 d).

Once you are holding the orbs, turn your palms to face each other, keeping them shoulder width apart. Do the hearts of the flowers reach for each other? Is there an attraction pulling your hands together?

Close your eyes and slowly move your hands towards each other until you sense a bounce of resistance. Open your eyes, keep your gaze soft and unfocused. What do you see or sense or imagine?

_____
_____
_____
_____
_____
_____
_____

Experience 71 Your Energetic Body - Energy Work

13

VENTURING INTO WILDISH

༄

13.1 Thin Places

You've felt it. Those times when you know one more step will take you past everything you've ever known. A slide to the left and you will slip through a crack—you will know for sure that every strange notion ever to float through your imagination will be proved real.

And, you stop. You freeze. Because, what if you are right?

Then you turn away, back towards the known, the safe. Even if it's an uncomfortable existence, you know the rules. You know that if you continue to do what you've always done, you will always achieve only what you already have. Do you want more? Do you want to know more about who you are, what your dreams and deep desires might look like if they were to be seen in the light? Can you bear to see? I'm going to help you soften into the experience.

Part of what I am teaching you in this book is the ability to create safe space for yourself. I want you to really allow yourself to enter into all my invitations on all the pages. I know it's difficult. I know it can be uncomfortable, and more than that. It can be rough. That's why being able to hold yourself, to understand what is sacred space, to know that YOU are the space that is holy is what gives you permission to be free.

Your base chakra is the red energy centre located at the base of your spine. This is where your emotional body anchors events and thought patterns related to survival and belonging.

Take a minute to visualise the colour red.

What are the first images that flash in your mind, the first sensations that roll through your belly when you think of this very particular colour? It's a simple question that's not so simple. Everyone's red will be different in shade, saturation, opacity, depth, texture. Are you someone who can taste the squashed berry, smell the bruised rose petal? Does the colour warm your cheeks with setting sunlight?

Red can be a confrontation; it is a call to belonging, an offering of deep nurturing—your mother's womb—the rust-coloured dirt of a desert that longs for a good wetting and bleeds freely with veins of flash flooding after a storm.

Red is the colour of ultimate safety and the essence of absolute security. It holds you. It takes you back to your first heartbeat and, literally, threads through your life.

Women have a naturally wildish nature that is strangled nicely over time, with the expertise of proper parenting and ingraining of classroom and workplace rules. Sometimes, the learning of these lessons is cruel. We live in a time now when the wild nature of Goddess and woman is breaking out. Whispers are becoming conversation, are becoming calls and song instead of only cries of mourning. I see her more and more often in the rebellious desire to simply take up space in the world. I see her looking out of the mirror at me; sometimes I glory in the reflection, sometimes I dive for the tweezers and pluck the hairs from my chin.

What I see makes me uncomfortable and I wonder what I'm so ashamed of. But wondering is a step beyond instinctive freezing. Daring to wonder means I am slipping through the clutching grasp of fear. I often wonder if I'm right, and everything I ever imagined winking and beckoning at me through the cracks is real.

Experience thin places

We're going to open your throat, get some sound passing over your tongue, breathe life into the music of your silence. This is probably going to be uncomfortable and I am smiling all over my face, darling one. We shall create some safe space for your practice first though. In fact, this section, whole, would make a wonderful ritual. Alone or in a sacred circle with trusted others, one day you might get wild and paint your soul red.

13.1 a) **Visualisation:** You can use this technique whenever you want to create safe space. Stand in the centre of the room you will be working in. Map out in your memory all the windows, doorways, hallway openings, stairwells, and skylights.

Turn in place, your gaze a laser beam tracking over all the surfaces of the room, building a model in your mind. When you are ready, close your eyes and see yourself exactly where you are in the centre of the model you have built in your imagination.

Chapter 13 ☙ Venturing Into Wildish

You are going to draw energetic curtains across all the openings into this room. Any place that could allow entry, you will draw a curtain over. From left to right, turning clockwise from the first instance, until you are done.

Imagine pulling a shimmering curtain shut, over each open space. Another time you may choose to make your energy curtains whatever colour seems most appropriate. This first time, make the cloth rich, deep red, shot through with a gold thread that reflects into the air around you. By the time you have finished closing all the curtains, your space is glimmering and burnished like a sorbet sunset.

Anything that would intend you harm or hurt cannot pass through these energetic boundaries. Should someone enter your space while the curtains are drawn, their bad juju will be swept from their shoulders as they walk through the curtains.

This is an excellent way to set up your office workspace.

To open the space once you are finished working, reverse the order of your visualisation. Open each curtain from right to left, turning anti-clockwise until you're back to the beginning again.

_____

_____

_____

_____

_____

Experience 72 Thin Places - Visualisation

13.1 b) **Chanting:** Base chakra tone and sound. The first thing I want you to do for this exercise is forget about doing it right. There is no right way to do this. There is your way. You might be sitting there giving me a mentally upthrust middle finger, with wide eyes and the knowledge that you can't sing to save yourself.

Nope. Nopedy nope. I disagree with your certainty. Perhaps someone once told you that you can't sing. What they meant was your singing didn't resonate to their scale. That's because your inner scale of tones is unique to you. I'm telling you, you can sing the heck out of those octaves.

I'm going to give you a resource to support this exploration of the innate melody of your chakra system. If you don't have an internet connection available, don't fret, I have some offline instructions to play with now. In fact, I encourage you to get into the offline part of the exercise first. The note that resonates with the base chakra is C. But that is not the only sound associated with that energy centre. And anyway, your interpretation of a C note is unique to you. Your intention to tune into that chakra is a powerful force. Magic is all about intention.

Remember the song from *The Sound of Music* called "Do Re Mi"? Perhaps there was a music teacher at school who used the words, do re mi fa so la ti to sing a scale to the class. Did you notice there are seven words in the scale? Seven tones to discover? The energy of your body threads through seven major chakras. Isn't that a delicious synchronicity?

The words for chanting into your chakras are: LAM, VAM, RAMM, YAM, HAM, OM, and AH (all pronounced with long vowels: A = Ah, O = Oh). We are going to start with the base chakra tone, LAM, to feel into the scale of your energetic body.

"LAM" is the word for your base chakra, the C note, the lowest note on your scale. Sing the word, "LAM" to yourself in the lowest note you are comfortable vocalising. Don't force your voice lower than it is comfortable going. Take a lovely, deep belly breath and just breathe out with your voice flowing as easily as the breath does. Fix your attention on your base chakra. Imagine the colour red flaring in time to your chanting. What do you know? You're singing in tune.

Let the sounds wash over you, get a sense of where the vibrations trill inside your body, focus on your base chakra. Open your mouth and breathe the sound of the vibration into your voice. If you find your throat becomes strained, your voice cramped, it's because you are disrespecting your personal boundaries. Rest when you know you need to rest; align your vocalisation to your own deepest note. Don't squash your awesomeness into someone else's construct of what is correct.

Journalling suggestion: Pick up your pen immediately while the last note of your chanting still hangs in the air, start writing into the space alive with your voice.

_____
_____
_____
_____
_____
_____
_____
_____
_____
_____
_____
_____
_____
_____

Experience 73 Thin Places - Chanting

13.1 c) **Playing:** Dress up, drape yourself in the red sheet you never use on the bed, pull on the crimson skirt that swirls out when you spin. Paint your face, your lips, your hands. Use the lip liner at the bottom of your makeup bag, the deep red that you used once, decorate your skin.

Maybe red lipstick is your thing already. Fab! Go nuts. Dare to take it past the edges of your lips.

What do you do next? Will your hips move of their own volition? Will you dance on the balls of your bare feet, spinning yourself dizzy, seducing your reflection with the beautiful undulations of your arms and hands? As

Part III 🌀 GERMINATE

you read this are you already belly breathing, is your soul moaning, sighing, vibrating?

Do this exercise following a base chakra toning session, then try it all by itself another time. The journalling that comes out of each will make interesting reading for contrast.

Journalling suggestion: Begin after your swirling dancing in exercise 13.1 c) ends, pick up your pen with hands that are stained and smeared with red. Let the pen swirl as you did, dot the page with fingerprints of red.

_____

_____

_____

_____

_____

_____

_____

_____

_____

_____

_____

_____

Experience 74 Thin Places - Playing

13.1 d) **Journalling:** I've provided space to write at the appropriate places mentioned in 13.1 Experience. I hope you try all the suggestions I offer in this exercise. Each time, your journalling will reveal surprises and secrets. I am so excited for your discoveries!

A final prompt: Allow the sensations and practices to soak into your being, go and shower, wrap up in your comfiest pyjamas—then write, draw into the afterglow.

Chapter 13 — Venturing Into Wildish

Experience 75 Thin Places - Journalling

13.2 Listening Through the Thinning

Every time you whisper a prayer while dangling from the end of your rope, wish for help, invoke your spirit guides, you are calling to your higher self. This is the part of you connected to All That Is. Stop for a moment and take a breath, I'll say it again.

It's you that is connected to All That Is: the impermanent, eternal, infinite Self of which you animate a spark. You are walking about inside an animated breath that the universe blew into existence.

You are that powerful.

Whether or not you allow the Divine to lead the way, it does.

When you meditate, you melt into that awareness. You loosen your focus on the dense matter your body bumps into, desires, attaches to and waft into the in between. It is there—outside of time, outside of space—that your randomly flung pleading transforms into its own answer.

Every time you ask a question of your spirit guide, ascended master, archangel, Jesus, medicine animal, Goddess, dead Great Aunt Agatha, you are calling out to You. Your intuition is the antenna for this vast web of information.

The Veil is called as such because it refers to the thin places. Thin places are where you disappear into the in between: a dip in the overgrown forest path that you traverse in three strides, only to pause at the far rise and blink at the return of nature's voices—birds, rustling leaves, a far-off dog barking. Something just happened and you have to pause to wonder before glancing over both shoulders, one at a time, giving a shudder. You shake it off and walk on. Or do you?

Perhaps your shivering form is the way you return from the place of mystery, fall through the other side of the Veil, soul becoming once more resonant with your physical body. So you close your eyes and stretch your senses out in an attempt to hold onto the tail of the moment, flickering at the edge of where your mind can make sense of reality. What if you could blend those edges and step through; what if you are the Veil that dulls your vision of the magic? Perhaps you are already smack dab in the middle of it all.

You can't do this wrong. The moment you decide to be present with the shudder of recognition, or continue to wander, or even quicken your pace to escape the chill (because why else would you be shivering?) remains—always was, is, will be—the perfect moment. Divine timing is exactly that. Divine. Just keep doing your thing, living your life.

Experience listening through the thinning

Let's get you outside the bounds of your edges, redefine your limits and transport your spirit to its place in the circle of your wise, higher mind. It's okay if you tell yourself this is imaginary. That doesn't mean it isn't real. Dreams of sleeping minds are as real as their plodding day doings. You are about to spend time with the pieces of you that you instinctively turn away from, the pieces that you reject, that literally make you sick.

13.2 a) **Meditation:** Find a comfortable place to sit, somewhere that feels cosy and where you won't be disturbed. Think nesting, or sheet and pillow forts you made as a child. That's the feeling you're aiming for. Once you've had some practice, you'll be able to tune into your spirit circle on the run. It becomes second nature. Their voices will start to replace the internal criticism that runs on a loop in your subconscious.

Close your eyes and snuggle in, get still and allow your breathing to deepen. Flow in and out with your breath. When your mind wanders, and it will, just come back to your breath.

Imagine your chair, the room, the building, the world falling away. Everything gets fuzzy at the edges and melts away to nothing.

Gently bring your surroundings back into focus. You are one of a group of beings in a circle. There may be many or few. Some of the faces you see clearly, some are indistinct, hooded, or concealed. Their voices might sound like the rustle of leaves, the growl of shifting rock, the groan of sun-kissed wood. Take your time.

The voices quiet and you feel drawn to speak into the silent questioning, to ask for direction. This is your space; use your own language and way of speaking. Yours are the magic words here and no other power is required.

Let the conversation run its course; you will know when it is time to return to your physical body. You can always begin the conversation by setting an intention. Something like, "When you have answered my question, please guide my spirit back to my body." Boundaries can create a sense of security, to allow you to fully relax.

_____

_____

_____

_____

_____

Part III 🌀 GERMINATE

Experience 76 Listening Through the Thinning - Meditation

13.2 b) **Healing:** Next time you go into spirit circle, take this with you: what gives you pain? Where in your body exists tension or discomfort? Is there a chronic pattern of dis-ease in your physical body that flares up regularly?

As soon as I asked the first question you knew the answer—the pain you need to work with right now made itself known. Don't dismiss it as not important or painful enough, too silly to give any time to, too complicated and systemic, hideously invasive to do anything about.

Talk with your circle about this pain, ask for direction, ask to remember their guidance once you've returned to your physical body. Your pain may become manifest in your spirit circle allowing you to have a direct conversation with it. Let your pain hold you, open your arms and invite it to be held. This is deep and vulnerable connection, and you are held safe in this sacred space.

Experience 77 Listening Through the Thinning - Healing

13.2 c) **Journalling:** Write out any instructions you were given in circle. Document your experience, the feelings, sensations, conversations, voices, connections, solace, distress. Were you in a room, deep in a wood, atop a mountain, no place, every place?

Part III GERMINATE

Experience 78 Listening Through the Thinning - Journalling

14
GROUNDING

14.1 Sensing Earth

You are human, part of the ever-evolving organism of this tiny blue ball spinning through space, which is part of a galactic body, the scope of which blows apart our meagre capacity for understanding infinity. That doesn't stop me from trying occasionally; I hope you attempt it every now and then, too.

As an integral part of this planetary organism, why do you think humans expend so much effort to separate themselves? Why is comfort bestowed by distancing from each other, from the ground that supports our steps? There is even prestige found in the elevation. Great stock is put in being more highly evolved in matters of spirit, gaining of material wealth, accumulation of knowledge. What nonsense. Where is the wisdom?

We are a physical body powered by electrical impulses, walking upon a world that generates the electricity that does the powering. When was the last time you took your shoes off to go outside?

Kicking off our shoes is the thing we do only after walking through the front door after a long day at work, at school, at wherever the busy place was you were. Even the time we take to go into the forest or park is spent shod by sturdy hiking boots, or rubber-soled sneakers.

Being permanently insulated from the power source that regulates and calibrates the equipment that supports our lives isn't logical. It's no wonder there are parts of us that feel like they are short-circuiting all the time—they are!

There is an intimate embrace awaiting your presence. The Earth herself constantly bares all for you. She holds nothing back and if you take the time to listen she'll tell you all her secrets, answer any question you ask, accept your deepest pain and transform it into wisdom.

Experience sensing earth

For this set of exercises, you will need to get outside. Your local park, wilderness, wooded walking trail. I took my own advice this past weekend. Walking through the forest at the end of our street, I delighted in the moment my girlfriend unlaced her shoes and stripped her socks to bare her soles to the winter earth.

Her whole expression melted into relief as the energetic medicine coursed through her body, yet I resisted. My hip ached, my gait became more lopsided, the earth said, "Really?" and laughed at my stubbornness. The instant I gave in and got some dirt on my skin my breath sucked in all the way through the soles of my feet. I felt gravity. My balance evened out. I felt the ache drawing from my hip, down into the earth. By the time I put my shoes back on, I was pain-free. True story.

14.1 a) **Grounding:** Take your shoes off and walk on the ground. This is the only instruction you need. The connection is instant.

Repeat daily.

Experience 79 Sensing Earth - Grounding

14.1 b) **Meditation:** Lie on the ground. Yes, head and all—get some grass and leaf tangled in your hair. Feel your spine against the earth; let her have your back. Close your eyes and soften into the feeling of being completely supported.

There is nothing more required of you than to be present. You don't have to earn this experience. You don't have to wait for permission. You are of earth, you are home.

Repeat often.

_____
_____
_____
_____
_____

Chapter 14  Grounding

_____
_____
_____
_____
_____
_____
_____
_____
_____
_____

Experience 80 Sensing Earth - Meditation

14.2 Reconnecting

We long for the unplugged vacation, to lose ourselves in no-time no-worry no-responsibility. Our circuits are overloaded with constant stimulation and over-charged desires for more. When you forget your phone I bet you feel a sharp jolt of (even momentary) distress. You might miss something… Or is that just me?

Losing connection with earth gives me headaches; my anchoring ribbons untie, I get floaty and feel disconnected from my life. I am naturally attuned to the element of air so it's easy to spend too much time in my thinking mind, fixing fixing fixing rather than flowing from a centred place. Planning escape routes is my vice.

The unplugged experience you crave is the polar opposite of disconnection. You long to belong, forgetting that you already do.

Experience reconnecting

I'm going to teach you how to remember your roots, how to walk through the world of earth and be connected with an entirely new social network. The deepening section will take you further than the meditation of exercise 14.1 b). You will curl up with underworld whispers, be held by the nourishing quiet, and listen with your whole body.

14.2 a) **Visualisation:** Get outside into the company of some trees. Take off your shoes, spend a few moments getting still and centred. Look around at the trees and plants, how their trunks and stems meet the ground, push into the dirt and grass.

Feel the place where your feet meet the ground. Push your own roots down into the dirt. Does the earth feel dry, moist, welcoming, resistant, soft?

Open your hands. Imagine long tendrils of draping roots coming from the tips of your fingers, growing longer and pushing into the earth. How deep do your roots extend? Do they go straight down or spread out into a wide mat beneath you?

Now, go for a walk. Your roots will flow through the earth as though it is fluid. Imagine them trailing through the ground beneath as you move. How does it feel? Take the time to feel all the way to the furry tip of every root.

The more you practise this exercise, the more easily you will put down your roots no matter where you are. Frustrating meeting on the twenty-sixth floor of your office building? No problem—put down your roots. That's the beauty of imagination, it takes you anywhere instantly and does the seemingly impossible when it arrives.

Experience 81 Reconnecting - Visualisation

14.2 b) **Deepening:** Outside with you! Lie on the ground as in exercise 14.1 b) and spend some time feeling the support of earth, drawing solidity and strength into your body.

Curl onto your side; pillow your cheek with your hands leaving your ear free to touch the ground. Close your eyes and listen. My favourite time of day to do this practice is dusk; the mystery of this turning time lends itself to the deepening.

Let your body grow heavy and imagine the ground sinks into a soft hollow. Feel how the earth holds you safe and murmurs as a mother would to a fractious baby. Listen to the language of stone, dirt, worms, beetles. Let the humming of grass roots brush over your consciousness.

The next time you have difficulty falling asleep, try this exercise curled on your side with the bed covers snuggled beneath your chin. Allow all the night noises to become far-off creaks and moans of deep shifting stone; let the earth sing you a lullaby.

Experience 82 Reconnecting - Deepening

15

TREE TALK

෧

15.1 Leaning in

I'm a reluctant tree-hugger. Does that amuse you? It sure tickles me. I'm the person who encourages everyone (in her mind and sometimes out loud) to get out and make friends with trees, rocks, lakes, random breezes.

In my core, I'm more of a tree-talker, tree-impressionist. A walk through the woods with me meanders from one side of the path to the other. Mostly you'll observe me watching the highest leaves and branches swaying as I seek the source of each rustle and creak. My girlfriend leads me around puddles and ditches; sometimes I even notice and thank her with a smile. As I've said before (have I?), air is my natural element. (I can't wait to write that experiential guide for you! But, that's a couple of books away yet—let's get back to earth.)

Some trees are inviting, they are playful and want to share their swaying dance with me. Yet most times I have to talk myself into stepping into their personal space. This attempt to impose human constructs on trees is laughable—and when I catch myself doing it, I chuckle. At least, I chuckle; sometimes I cackle. I think it has something to do with the phase of the moon.

Before I've convinced myself to physically connect with a tree, I look for its face. They all have a face, sometimes several. If I can't locate its face I listen, I lean a hand or a cheek against its bark and listen. Like radar, my senses scoot up the trunk and flare in the canopy to capture the slow groans and slight moans of movement.

I love the way my girlfriend leans into the curves of a tree, embraces the whole trunk with the huge reach of her tiny frame. She knows how to embody earth instinctively, understands the flowing language of sap. Me? I gaze longingly at the high places and wish myself into the branches with the wild-looking crow's nest.

There are so many languages in the world, most of them non-human. Tree talk. The patient existence of grass. Lie on the lawn sometime; imagine the sleepy murmurs that fill the tough roots of grass. The way slight green blades spring back up despite drought and deluge seems dreamy rather than determined. The reality of grass ignores what humans consider damaging and just gets on with living. It must be a murmuring type of communication—a never-ceasing croon to the possibility of existence.

Experience leaning in

Once you step over the threshold of possibility, there is no going back. One conscious footstep into magic and you begin to notice, continue to notice, cannot help but see. Every action bulges with the potential for adventure.

15.1 a) **Listening:** Go outside and find a tree whose trunk is at least the thickness of your body. When you spot the one you want to do this exercise with, stop moving and focus your attention on it. Take in its whole form, from roots to canopy. Be still and imagine the focus you are holding is a tangible thing connecting you with the tree, the tree with you. Is the connection gossamer, cords, light, lines of music from a song you haven't thought of in ages? How is the tree calling to you?

Make your way towards the tree. Take your time.

Place your palms against the bark. This might be as far as you are able to sustain this exercise the first time you attempt it. That's okay—I'm with you. Just be in the moment and witness what is going on. Stay with it even if it feels strange.

Place your hands at face-height to cushion your cheeks, then lean your forehead against the bark. How does it feel? Like a bow, a wondering, a request, restful, secret?

Are your eyes closed? Can you open them? Try both ways (eyes open and closed) and take time to be in each way of existing for a few moments. Notice!

Focus in, imagine your way to the other side of the bark. Slide your awareness into the centre of a knot or bulge in the trunk until you are on

Chapter 15 Tree Talk

the inside. Listen; soak up every murmur and creak and hushing wash of sap.

_____
_____
_____
_____
_____
_____
_____
_____
_____
_____

Experience 83 Leaning In - Listening

15.1 b) **Embodying:** Turn and lean back against the trunk. Place your feet between the tree's roots. If you can't see any roots imagine your feet are with them beneath the ground.

Lean against different sections of the trunk until you find the place that best fits your curves. Maybe you can't find a fitting place; you feel you don't fit at all, making you hyperaware of your connection. That's okay.

Remember, this is not the only tree you can invite to be part of this experience. This is not a one-time happening. Embodying earth is something you do now; you won't be able to help yourself. You've no idea how that idea makes me grin!

Lean your head back against the trunk, gaze up into the branches. Imagine your arms are branches, your fingers, leaves or twigs.

Stretch your arms up and copy the movements of the branches above you. Did you dare to branch out? Are you here with yourself and your experience, or divided? What causes the division if it exists?

_____
_____
_____
_____
_____
_____
_____
_____
_____
_____
_____
_____

Experience 84 Leaning In - Embodying

15.2 Leaning Intimately

Demonstrating how to lean into the curves of your physical body, your soul-body, is as instinctive to me as tree hugging is to my girlfriend. Encouraging you to look inside, holding you while you listen to your heartbeat is my gift, and ultimately yours. Supporting you inside the space where self-talk overwhelms your ability to remain upright, gentling your inner dialogue into new ways of kindness and possibility is why I do this work.

When was the last time you touched yourself with love? I know where your imagination zinged to when you read that last sentence, it's precisely why I asked the question.

For that matter, when was the last time you masturbated with an intimate sense of self-connection? That's a whole other book; yes really, a whole book. I have plans! But, think about it. Even pleasuring yourself, an act you associate with the word intimate (as you should), is something people separate themselves from: denying the act itself, denying the power of that connection. There is no intimacy in the thing you call masturbation when you smother the whispered words behind shame in the secret back room of your hidden conversations with self.

I'll rephrase the question. When was the last time you wrapped your arms around yourself with real affection? Trailed your fingertips across the skin of your arm, breathed in the scent of your sun-soaked hair? More of this in that other book I mentioned.

Does this whole notion of paying attention to your physical form make you squirm? There is a delicate beauty to the armour of numbed emotion we carve into our beautiful bodies. Self-protection is awesome in its ability to appear lovely and pathetic. Its necessity is so apparent.

Experience leaning intimately

First thing: don't panic. I promise to stay with you through this whole book. I've been here to this point and I'll be here with you each time you gaze into the pages and meet me between the words.

Something I treasure about working in the field of energy medicine is exactly that—it doesn't matter where you are, or when you sit in these experiences—I am here with you. You are my focus, as I write this, as you read this. We are sharing the same moment. I am the invisible whisper of safety you long for.

15.2 a)   **Listening:** You are going to lean into your body, take a step towards kindness and self-love. You are also going to do this exercise nude.

What do you feel, having just read that last instruction? Did you immediately discount it as a possibility? This is not suggestion for titillation, this is you learning to be with yourself, to take up the same space as your body, to centre.

It's okay to feel awkward or silly, meeting someone for the first time can often be like that. Keep breathing. Keep blinking.

When you have taken off your clothes, stand in the centre of your space with your legs hip-width apart. Extend your arms away from your sides just enough that they lose contact with your torso.

Close your eyes. Imagine an outline being traced around your entire form, all the way around—beneath your feet and above your head, in front and behind. Within this cocoon, the noises of your body begin to amplify.

The cocoon of your imagining captures all the gurgles, thumps, pops, and whooshes for your exploration. Take your time. You are an observer for this exercise, there is no other instruction. Stay here and listen to your body.

Experience 85 Leaning Intimately - Listening

15.2 b) **Journalling:** Get dressed. Record your experience. Take some brief notes if you feel unable to immediately go deep. Come back to your notes later and flesh them out. It's important to journal straight away; you think you'll remember, but the sensations will fade. You will hide from yourself.

Perhaps the next time you do this practice you will expand on the notes, or take entirely new notes. Remember, journalling can take many different forms. Draw, paint, video, write, whatever method you use is perfect.

_____

_____

_____

_____

Chapter 15 — Tree Talk

_____
_____
_____
_____
_____
_____
_____
_____
_____
_____
_____

Experience 86 Leaning Intimately - Journalling

15.2 c) **Embodying:** Do the exercise as described above in 15.2 a) in front of a mirror.

When you imagine the outline being traced around your body, include your reflection as an extension of your form. So, the outline will go all around your body, beneath your feet and above your head, then over your reflection's head and behind, all around her body, beneath her feet. You are both inside the cocoon.

What is being amplified now?

Can you bring your focus to the sounds of your body, the whispers of its proof of function? When critical self-talk hijacks this exercise—and it will—close your eyes, breathe, and refocus on the sounds of your body.

Experience 87 Leaning Intimately - Embodying

15.2 d) **Journalling:** Wrap yourself in a soft sheet, blanket, robe. Record your experience. Please. Let the words or images flow onto your pages. Everything is allowed in your journalling.

This is the vent, the release valve, the nonsense on your way to more nonsense (more than likely). But once it's on the page, you can take a good look at it. When it stays in your head, the form shifts, the words blur and change.

_____
_____
_____
_____
_____
_____
_____
_____

Chapter 15 ⁷ Tree Talk

_____ Draw your experience →

Part III GERMINATE

Use this blank space to draw your experience.

Experience 88 Leaning Intimately - Journalling

PART IV

SPROUT

"Throw your dreams into space like a kite, and you do not know what it will bring back, a new life, a new friend, a new love, a new country."
—Anaïs Nin

16

BELIEVING IN POSSIBILITY

༉

16.1 Breathing Into the Quote

Following is the quote and meditation that frames this part.

> *"Throw your dreams into space like a kite, and you do not know what it will bring back, a new life, a new friend, a new love, a new country."* –Anaïs Nin

Just before turning forty, I did something I never imagined I would do. I broke my life.

The breath I took immediately after voicing the desire to not be married anymore was so deep it plunged into the centre of the earth. It breathed me. I didn't have a clue what my dreams were anymore, but nothing was ever going to be the same again.

Possibility is like that—unknown, terrifying, profoundly peaceful.

There was so much wonderful space in that place, that wormhole that opened up and swallowed me whole. It might have been easy to mistake the sensation I felt as one of being disconnected. That might have been my instant assumption. After all, disconnection from an event with the potential to be the most disturbing and confronting of my life sounds like self-preservation 101. Except, I know what disconnection feels like. I have years of experience. A lifetime of practical implementation. This was not that.

The first time you deliberately turn away from an initial instinct to ask permission is precious. It is the first delicate tendril of green pushing through the darkness, it is your brokenness searching for light on the surface.

Part IV 𐂊 SPROUT

But first, your seed had to crack. The husk had to split, be saturated, spark to the possibility.

You don't know, can't know what will happen next. I love that.

Experience believing in possibility

Holding too tightly to dreams crushes them before they have the chance to fly. Because, what if… Fill in the blank. "What if" needs to take on a more daring tone in your imagination. Shake off the shivering, speak through the quavering of your voice, say the words even though they make no sense—yet. That's the whole point of what ifs.

16.1 a) **Contemplation:** Sit with the words of this section's quote. Take the time to feel all the ways it makes you feel. Journal your contemplation. What are the limits that spring up to fend off possibility, to hobble all the what if kites your dreams awaken in your inner critic?

_____
_____
_____
_____
_____
_____
_____
_____
_____
_____
_____
_____
_____
_____

Experience 89 Believing in Possibility - Contemplation

Chapter 16 — Believing in Possibility

16.1 b) **Journalling:** Pick the dream that is the most impossible. Tell me why it is impossible. Write me a letter:

"Dear Sondra, my most impossible dream is…

"It's impossible because…"

Justify your beautiful heart out.

_____
_____
_____
_____
_____
_____
_____
_____
_____
_____
_____
_____
_____
_____
_____
_____
_____
_____
_____
_____

Experience 90 Believing in Possibility - Journalling

Part IV SPROUT

16.1 c) **Playing:** Get a pen, a marker, something that will write on anything. Go outside, find a place where there are lots of leaves, or pebbles, or bits of bark strewn over the ground.

Collect three of the leaves, pebbles, or bits of bark. Write one word on each that represents one dream you have.

Close your eyes, breathe deeply, fill your collection of dreams with the energy of possibility. One at a time, throw each dream away: over your shoulder, baseball pitcher style with an excellent and furious round up, under hand and gentle.

Don't look for them.

I wonder which dream will stick in your mind, tuck into your heart, and come home with you.

Experience 91 Believing in Possibility - Playing

17

TOO COMMON TO COUNT

17.1 Invisibility

Staying invisible is a survival tactic. I understand it. I've used it. It takes support and courage to step into the light. One toe in the sun and we might explode into a thousand pieces. How amazing would that be? Dig down into your compacted plant pot and tell me that it isn't precisely what you need.

Becoming visible is an incredible action; it's much quieter than I had anticipated. It's anticlimactic in the best possible way.

Becoming visible happens when you start to tell the truth. You begin to see yourself—this was never about anyone else seeing you. Most people will always see you the way they are, with little regard to how you are. They see you through their filters the same way you see them through your filters. It's a shadowy, shaded existence, my darling.

When my girlfriend and I walk in the forest it's a moving meditation. We are offended by loud conversations, let alone motorbikes ripping through.

She's tried to teach me how to fade, how to be a tree, how to be invisible. But this is not the same kind of invisibility I was talking about before. This is shape-shifting. There is a softening inward, a rippling outward to merge energy, morph my perception of my outsides to match the environment.

I can do it if I move away from all the well-worn paths, am very still and concentrate. She can do it on the move, walking beside me. I swear—she vanishes.

I've only seen deer on two occasions. Once was as I shifted back into my own form after being a tree for a while. The other was on a particularly otherworldly day when the mist made me feel like I was walking through a sky forest, and the deer was bounding away from us in the distance.

It's evidence of our different aptitudes for shape-shifting that she often comes home from a lone walk in the woods to tell me about coming face to face with a deer, remaining with each other in a few moments of suspended surprise at the other being there.

I am impatient. I feel connected to the dove, which is what people here in the Netherlands call a pigeon: an ordinary old pigeon. I am too common to count.

Yet, when I allow my preconceptions to fall away and fade towards a dove I see rainbows in her feathers, pink sunsets, amethyst comfort. I hear her crooning moonstone invitation to be exactly who I am.

Perhaps that's why I reject the connection. I don't want to be common. But I don't want to be so noticeable I seem dangerous, which makes me a target: childhood conditioning that seeps through into moments of my grown-arse life. I'm still learning that it's perfect to just be me. Just like you.

So often the tree in which a dove perches shows a face that rolls its eyes, quirks the right side of its top lip up in soundless amusement at my unspoken palaver. Trees are part of my extended support network, my prodders and pokers, my darers of the next do. Patience is their most powerful tool.

Experience invisibility

It's time to consider what elements of earth, animals, sensations, sounds you feel a particular connection with. Have you ever thought about it? Make that consideration a layer of this experience. Notice what you are drawn to during your practice; turn towards each prompting rather than deciding it's not supposed to be part of your experience. Take the time to research the energy medicine of the animal or tree that drew you.

17.1 a)   **Moving meditation:** Find some woodland and walk in it. Take each step deliberately, see everything that comes in front of your eyes, register all the scents that swirl into your nostrils, and notice what they taste like in the back of your throat.

Go by yourself. This part of the instruction might be the most difficult. Go by yourself, be with yourself, take yourself out of your everyday automation and tell the people around you that you are going. You are going and they can't come with you—say that right out loud.

Woodland might simply mean your local park, don't make the fact that you live in a city an excuse or hindrance.

Chapter 18 🌀 Shifting Reality

_____
_____
_____
_____
_____
_____
_____
_____
_____
_____

Experience 92 Invisibility - Moving Meditation

17.1 b) **Visualisation:** Seeing tree faces and plant spirits is something you will forever, now, do automatically. It's actually more of a relaxation than action, but requires more than softening your gaze.

You need to shimmer into that alone time that a lifetime of classroom teachers either forbade you to enter, or jerked you out of. That daydream state of melting mind, melding mind. The alone time where the hidden meaning of the word "alone" reveals itself. The word stretches enough to allow an extra letter l, and you enter a space where "all one" is the way of understanding more than your thought you knew.

Choose a tree, or plant. Lovely, large trees with broad, gnarled trunks are wonderful to begin this practice with. They have so much character worn into their surface, poking out from their insides, you could believe yourself to contain not an ounce of imagination and still see a face in this kind of tree trunk.

The first few times you practise this exercise, stand still, find a balance, feel the earth beneath your feet holding you. Then, begin to soften your gaze and slow your breathing. Sink deeper into both sight and breath. Head towards the sinking feeling: that delicious sleepy, drifting out the classroom window sensation.

Part IV 🌱 SPROUT

Here is my most important instruction for this visualisation: believe what you see.

_____
_____
_____
_____
_____
_____
_____
_____
_____

Experience 93 Invisibility - Visualisation

17.1 c) **Shape-shifting:** Becoming invisible—this wisdom is gifted to us by the instinctive shaman, who is my girlfriend.

"You have a shape, everything exists of molecules. Everything is like that: trees, rocks, the buzzard calling to me while she catches a warm updraft over the forest. Let your molecules, which you imagine are tightly bound, expand. Create space between them. Imagine the same expansion is happening to the spaces between the molecules of the forest, all it contains, and allow everything to merge.

"I am one, we are one.

"Expand. Create space and invite in what is around you.

"The molecules shift, expand, leaving room for the forest to pass through you. You lose your edges, you and the forest blend.

"When I am feeling resistant to instinctive shape-shifting, I recite, 'Earth is my body, water is my blood, air is my breath.' At this point I can feel myself expanding, can feel the air in my hair, on my skin, going through me. I AM earth, I AM water. 'Fire is my spirit' is the last phase of the chant, but I don't usually get to that. I also say, 'As outside, so inside.' And then, the forest is in me, I'm walking through myself."

Chapter 18 Shifting Reality

Now, lovelies, there is some soul-felt magic for you to embody.

_____
_____
_____
_____
_____
_____
_____
_____

Experience 94 Invisibility - Shape-shifting

Embodying chant

Earth is my body,
Water is my blood,
Air is my breath,
Fire is my spirit.

Blending chants

I am one, we are one.

As outside, so inside.

When you say these phrases, focus your energy. Let it build in your low belly, as though you are cultivating the intense purr of a lioness, who knows she is precisely where she is meant to be. When you speak the words, let them come from that low belly power point. Let the words be part of your walk, part of your earth connection; feel the strength in your legs, the soles of your feet.

Experience 95 Invisibility - Chanting

18

SHIFTING REALITY

18.1 The Possibility of New Direction

It's synchronistic, to say the least, that I'm writing about changing directions and shifting reality on this particular morning. I'm in recovery. If I were speaking to anyone else but you I would say I'm recovering from a long-standing pelvic injury. Properly named, it's more of a condition than an injury—but there I go, speaking to strangers again. And you're not that.

I'll tell you the truth. I'll do this telling because I need to get it out of my head, out from behind the blockage I've reinforced over the years, out of the dark. First I have to go into the shadow though. Come with me? It might be that we only dip our toes into the shade. It might be that the shadows are completely different to how you've always judged them to be, and only variations of light after all.

I tend to unpick any physical distress from the emotional and spiritual sides first. Well, after I stop grimacing and moaning, it's the place I automatically go to. Leaving the core of emotional dis-ease in the shadow of a physical injury or pain keeps the ground fertilised for the next season of that particular wound—the next trigger, reminder. The next time I turn away from myself, break a promise to my body, ignore her cries.

Stepping into the wavering in-between dimensions of my magical reality affords me shifted perspectives from which to view the injury, pick the scabs, watch the blood bead. It is the sacred space I've spoken about in earlier sections of this guide, that in between. And it's always with you, around you, is you. It's a blink or breath on the other side of your certainty that this moment of pain and distress will last for the rest of your life.

If I turn towards this pain I'm feeling, if I open to the possibilities it offers, I must rethink my original disclaimer of it being a condition, not an injury. This is an injury of my spirit; it's a soul wound that has waited patiently, gathering strength in the shadows of my emotional body until it had power enough to burst through my deliberate ignorance and blast its wisdom into my physical existence.

There is a balance to be found. Perhaps I have been out of balance for so long, it will be difficult to recognise what true balance looks like, feels like. Perhaps this searching is the balance. Flowing between possibilities and dimensions free of judgement that whatever way I am should be anything other than what it is.

Experience the possibility of new direction

This experience will take you inside yourself. You probably think of yourself as a cohesive animal: you have presence; you can see a reflection in the mirror when you brush your teeth. Let's get you seeing your insides and other hidden dimensions as easily as you do your outsides. You are a collective of parallel existences. The dimension we are going to work with in this experience is your emotional realm.

18.1 a)   **Relaxation:** This is the right time for you to get your candles and potions out. Get all woohoo for me, for yourself; do only the things that stir your curiosity—ever. You are your own guru.

Drip one or two drops of sandalwood essential oil onto the wax around the wick of your candle. Among other things, sandalwood helps sluggish energy stir and shift, and strengthens your sense of peace. Take time to just be with this part of the exercise. The oil will aid your patience; it is naturally slow moving. Like humans, sandalwood essential oil likes to be warmed up before working; you might give the bottle a soak in hot water first. Build your own ritual, lovely one.

Light the candle. I like to use a match and make the act part of the magic: the striking, spiking of the flame, snuffing out, watching the furl of smoke as the heat dissipates.

Sit back and watch the flame. Wait and soften as the scent of sandalwood surrounds you. Go where the scent takes you. Imagine the glow of the candle's flame expands until that is all there is. Imagine you are the glow combined with the warm, woody scent of the essential oil. It is you and you are it.

Chapter 18 Shifting Reality

The following meditation would be delicious to flow on with, right now.

Experience 96 The Possibility of New Direction - Relaxation

18.1 b) **Meditation:** Flow this meditation on from the previous exercise, or find somewhere comfortable to sit and get yourself centred with some slow, full breathing. Close your eyes while you settle in, you'll feel yourself growing heavier as you sink into your meditative space.

If you've been practising all (or even some) of the exercises in this guide, you will be getting comfortable with the notion of "settling in" and creating sacred space for meditation.

Set an intention for this meditation. Use your own words to guide what will follow:

"The purpose of this meditation is to meet my emotional body."

"I intend to explore my emotional body."

"I want to explore my emotional landscape."

Allow your attention to drift. Let it be like a mote of dust swirling through your body.

Notice. Is it dark or light on the inside of you? Are there patches of colour or shadow? Where does the mote of your attention spin in place, get stuck, completely avoid? It is quiet or is there a hum of ethereal melody? Are you transported to a landscape, complete with overgrown jungle vine, or desolate wind-carved sand dunes?

When you're ready to return to full consciousness, take your time to come back. Wiggle your fingers and toes, move your tongue around inside your mouth, roll your shoulders; fit your body back around your spirit like you are shrugging yourself into a jacket. I wonder, is your jacket well-worn and comfy, or tight, or threadbare?

_____

_____

_____

_____

Part IV SPROUT

_____
_____
_____
_____
_____
_____
_____
_____
_____

Experience 97 The Possibility of New Direction - Meditation

18.2 Balance and Believing

Ultimately, balance is the way of life. No matter how far in one direction the pendulum of existence swings, it will arc back the other way in equal measure. This is law. It is also true that ours is an ever-expanding universe; movement is… It just is. And so, seeking to still the pendulum in the vertical position is futile. Better to learn how to sway your hips in time with its graceful curves.

That arc you inscribe between pendulum extremes is the measure of your boundary. Most of the time, we think a boundary is an enclosed space, but in this case it means the extents to which you would dare: the tipping point of imagination where nonsense begins to make the most sense of all.

Can you imagine yourself running up the slope of your pendulum's curve, just making it to the end and grabbing on with both hands for all you're worth so you don't fly off into the deep dark of the unknown? Can you feel the relief of dangling for a moment, before swinging to build sufficient momentum to make it back, cupping your palms over the slippery spiritual zip line and whooshing back to centre?

In mythology and literature, the Lord and Lady are one representation of the balance inherent to all of existence. There are moments, aeons, millennia dotted through history when one or the other outshone, shot down, the other. We are heading towards a narrowing of the arc where polarities spin towards each other for a more intimate and vulnerable embrace rather than repelling, rather than needing the other to be less, or more, or even equal. Two forces of equal magnitude are just as capable of being ever apart as being clamped together.

My daughters, born in 1998 and 2001, who are now twenty and sixteen years old, are shining examples of the current course of reality's swing. Well, my reality, anyway. Gender lines, so adamantly and furiously carved into the bedrock of a society taught that restriction is the only way to fit in, are being eroded with every scrape of the oscillating desire of a new generation to just get over all the bullshit and get real.

Perhaps the ideal case is one not of narrowing the arc, but lifting the other extreme up into the swing and flying together. We are heading into a time where the other is all of us, and therefore none of us.

Remember, feeling off-centre is only one point in the arc of the swing. It means you are on your way back through. Your soul knows the way: lean back, hold on, and fly!

What is it that you believe? You might notice that you have multiple sets of parameters with which you determine believability. There is the reality you acknowledge on an everyday basis, and the expanded realities that you soften into when you are in spiritual practice, lost in daydream, soaking in the bath, on the edge of sleep.

Experience balance and believing

Make the three exercises of this experience that of taking yourself out for a date, a getting to know each other again or maybe for the first time.

18.2 a) **Contemplation:** Central to any ritual is your approach to the doing of it, your intention. I want you to feel held on solid ground for this exercise, so go outside and lay on the ground: in your backyard on the lawn, in the park on the grassy slope of a hill. This exercise is called a contemplation, you might also call it pure daydreaming.

Press your palms to the ground. Connect with your spine and feel the way the ground comes up to meet your body. Scan around your body and relax any tight places: your shoulders, your pelvis, and thighs. Let your whole body become heavy; imagine it has sunk into the ground a fraction.

When you are ready, ask yourself the following questions:

What does balance look like, feel like for you?

_____

_____

_____

_____

_____

How do you know when you are out of balance?

_____

_____

_____

_____

_____

Is there a particular imbalance that you avoid thinking about? Why is that?

_____
_____
_____
_____
_____
_____
_____
_____
_____

Each time you do this practice it will be different and there is no time limit, leave your watch at home. In fact, if you are feeling particularly brave, leave your phone at home, too.

When you are finished, call your spirit back into your body. Feel the blades of grass against your skin, wriggle your body slightly, and roll from one side to the other.

Experience 98 Balance and Believing - Contemplation

18.2 b) **Embodying:** Rise up from the ground; stand evenly on your soles, bare feet get bonus points. Move your body with the curve of your contemplation, the to and fro of the balance you've been exploring. Rest each palm on a curve of your body; let them cup the curves while you rock your body to match the sensation of the curve. Turn. Raise your arms over your head and touch the backs of your hands together, float your hands back to the curve of your body. You are dancing your curves.

Do this exercise even if you think it's stupid, pointless, hard—especially then.

Experience 99 Balance and Believing - Embodying

18.2 c) **Playing:** Chances are there is a playground or public park not far from exactly where you are right now. Chances are, there is a big set of swings waiting for you.

You already know exactly how to fly; you just haven't practised for a good long while. Here are your pre-flight instructions: feel everything, on the outside of your skin and on the inside of your mind.

Get to it.

Experience 100 Balance and Believing - Playing

19

ARE YOU READY?

19.1 Asking for Help

Win is the name of one of the supporting characters in Affery's Earth because the Old English meaning of win is *elf or magical being, friend*, and my character is all of those things. Part of the magic of helpers is that they turn up in our lives exactly when we need them, not when we want them.

Healthy dependence is not weakness. One can be independent and also need help. Acknowledging the moment, the time to ask for support, is the key to unlocking the power of the act. Vulnerability asks us to just be with it, in that space of not knowing. You don't have to know all the time. Really, you don't.

Hearing the answers that you've asked for is also a powerful piece of magic. How many times have you asked with no intention of hearing the response? You've asked because it was the way out of a situation that was growing far too close, your shields were weakening; they mustn't see through. Your questions were intended to throw them off the scent, not bring them closer.

Even if you do hear the answer, how hard have you fought to avoid receiving it? Because the answer is not elegant, you know better—or you don't know better but this is getting weird and uncomfortable.

Being ready to request, hear, and receive help often happens at the point of desperation, once all disguise has been stripped away. Sometimes life blows up in our faces and asking for help feels like the only option, but it also feels like the worst possible solution. It's a declaration of failure—at first. With the gaining of wisdom comes the understanding that it's actually a declaration of trust, which is strength of heart: a heart strong enough to simply be. What a beautiful thing.

When I shout out to the universe, plead for the reasons why, I'm always offered an answer. But, like breaking promises to myself, ignoring the proffered answers is all too easy. It's a good thing life is patient. Well, it's patient, but there comes a time when the metaphorical rug is ripped from beneath my plodding feet and I'm sent tumbling into the unwanted. Can you tell it's happened to me more than once? Is it the same for you, too?

Experience asking for help

Trusting yourself enough to believe the answers that bubble up into your conscious mind is a heart connection worth cultivating. Yours is a voice of wisdom. Do you believe me?

19.1 a) **Journalling:** For each of the prompts:

Write the question in your workbook (ask).

Sit with the question, get soft, call on your deeper self (hear).

Disengage your internal critic and let the answer flow through your pen (receive).

For each prompt, write about a specific event.

Explore how you felt then, feel now, how you were or were not changed by the event, why you think you are recalling this event at this time.

Prompt A: How readily do you accept help?

_____

_____

_____

_____

_____

_____

_____

Chapter 19 Are You Ready?

Prompt B: How generously do you extend help?

Part IV SPROUT

Prompt C: Can you remember a time you had the rug pulled out from under you?

Experience 101 Asking for Help - Journalling

19.2 Spirals

Life is not a straight line between birth and death. Every moment is a winding and unwinding experience of cycles and seasons. No matter where I turn, I am eternally cycling back to Self. This is the universal labyrinth that we, all unconscious, walk until we begin to see the path. Then, we still walk.

Have you ever had to untangle a ball of yarn? Labyrinth work is a bit like that—if you do it right. Oh, who am I kidding? There is no way for you to do it wrong. Even if you begin with a smoothly wound skein, one journey to the centre of a labyrinth, any labyrinth, will see you tied and beautifully tangled.

You might think that to backtrack, retrace your steps—which is what you seem to do when traversing a labyrinth—will set you to rights. Nope. Life can't be undone, only experienced. Are you here, with your life, right now? Are you completely here with me and the words on the page in front of you?

The more determined my pursuit of a goal, the more knots I create in my single-minded hunt. I am deaf to sounds of delight, blind to the wonder of the experience itself. The journey is not taken to reach the goal. Magic is missed when I decide that my interpretation of best outcome is the right one. There is no right way or certain destination—only the journey.

Experience spirals

Can you let the spirals take you? This is your practice for sensing, seasoning the surface of your path. Even falling off the edges of your path is still the path.

19.2 a) **Moving meditation:** Go to your favourite wooded area, it will be your labyrinth for this exercise. Follow the worn paths and, for the first section of time, turn right at the intersections that call your attention. For the second section of time, take all left-hand turns to make your way back to the beginning.

Take responsibility for your safety. Do this meditation in a place with which you are familiar and will be able to navigate your way out of with little hesitation.

_____

_____

_____

_____

Experience 102 Spirals - Moving Meditation

19.2 b) **Contemplation:** There is a pattern in your life that you keep repeating. Each time you feel you have completed the cycle it becomes more intimate, more personal, more intense.

Take a large sheet of paper and a pen. Place the tip of the pen at the centre of the page, spiral a line out to the edge and once there, spiral your way back into the centre.

Which life pattern emerges as the one ripe for contemplation today? Take the first one that bubbles up from the whirlpool of your spiralling lines. Put down your pen, soften your gaze, sink into the centre of the spiral and see where it takes you.

Experience 103 Spirals - Contemplation

19.2 c) **Journalling:** I encourage you to journal your experience of the contemplation in this section. Over time, you'll become familiar with your patterns and learn how to hold them with gratitude.

Chapter 19 ❡ Are You Ready?

_____
_____
_____
_____
_____
_____
_____
_____
_____
_____
_____

Experience 104 Spirals - Journalling

19.3 Base Chakra

Typically, you will be told that your base chakra is the energy centre located at the base of your spine. I want to expand your notions. While your root chakra does extend into the first few vertebrae of your spine, this rich, red, energy vortex is also cradled between your thighs; it swirls its spiral against your perineum, connecting you and grounding you in this physical world.

In matters of security and safety, physical identity, foundational support in this life, your base chakra is the doorway through which the red thread winds. Thoughts of pure survival throb here, pull your anus tight when fear flashes through your being.

When something is described as base it frames the thing as undesirable, unworthy, sordid, dirty, mean. Is it any wonder our base chakras get crunchy with neglect and need? Take a moment to consider: did you read the word base and immediately thought of a strong foundation?

Your physical body is a wonder. Your existence is welcome; you have a right to be. No matter what doubts you may have buried inside events from infancy and childhood about your utter magnificence, I'm telling you, you can love yourself through all of that.

Experience your base chakra

Let's get earthy and solid with this one. When I say the words chakra and energy, you probably don't think of anything you can touch. I want to turn that thought upside down. You are going to want to create some privacy for the final section of this experience—it's okay, trust me, trust yourself.

19.3 a) **Contemplation:** Make sure you have time to include exercise 19.3 b) to follow on directly from this contemplation. <u>This is important</u>. Please experience the contemplation and release together.

What situation from your past bubbles up when you think about the word "abandoned?" Allow yourself to sit with the situation, be kind with yourself while you do. You don't need to do anything, just hold yourself to the thought. There is nothing to fix or remedy.

Move on to the second part of this exercise, to experience release when you are ready. <u>Don't end the experience here</u>.

Experience 105 Base Chakra - Contemplation

19.3 b) **Release:** Go outside and sit on the ground. Settle in (you know how that goes) and breathe for a while, just be part of the world and realise you aren't taking up space but are interconnected with every part of existence. It is impossible for the universe to exist without you in it.

Bring to mind the subject of your contemplation for this section. Let it float around inside your imagination.

Focus on the place your backside connects with the Earth. Imagine the ground under you softening slightly. It takes on a fluid quality and begins to swirl slowly around the point of your perineum.

Direct the doubt from your contemplation to flow from your head, down your spine, and into the swirling earth.

Allow the doubt to be sucked away and transformed into mulch for your growth. You are growing a strong foundation of trust.

_____
_____
_____
_____
_____
_____
_____
_____
_____
_____
_____
_____
_____
_____
_____

Experience 106 Base Chakra - Release

19.3 c) **Connecting:** Go into the bedroom and lock the door. Choose a time when there won't be little fists banging on the door, or people calling for your attention. It's phone off the hook time.

No rushing is allowed. Get undressed, get your beautiful body balanced on both feet and just stand there for a few minutes.

Everything is energy. Every. Thing. Bid welcome to your existence, your right to be, the wonder of your physical body.

Touch the pads of your fingers to your perineum: the couple of centimetres of delicate skin between your scrotum or vaginal opening, and anus. As you do, realise that you are cupping not only your body, but your base chakra, also. Can you sense your more than physical body within the hold of your hand?

What do you feel? Curious? Uncomfortable? Aroused? Awkward? Tingly? Embarrassed? Nothing? Take your time—trust, stay with yourself for more time than you think you are able to allow. Just be here and experience a greater dimension of you.

_____
_____
_____
_____
_____
_____
_____
_____
_____
_____
_____
_____
_____
_____

Chapter 19 — Are You Ready?

Experience 107 Base Chakra - Connecting

20
RESISTING CHANGE

20.1 FEAR OF FALLING

Sometimes my resistance to change is magnificent. At the core of my fear to change is not failing, but disappointing. Disappointing me is not a consideration, not in that moment my foot hovers above the brink. Even within the last breath I take before nothing is the same again, my concern is for everyone but me. Shouldn't I make an appearance, too?

This person for whom I'm holding my breath isn't one person; they are an amalgam of every powerful voice I've absorbed. The initial experience of those separate sources wasn't necessarily negative. Perhaps that's what makes them so overwhelmingly important to impress. To disappoint them would show that I'm not worthy of whatever approval I previously received.

It's vital I impress this person; it's so imperative that the possibility of failing to do so becomes a knot in my gut that makes me physically sick. Yet, they may not be someone who currently takes up any space in my real life. It's all in my head.

What do you know? It is a fear of failing—failing to be the same way I was, back then when I impressed them. If that's the measuring stick, we are all failing, every moment of our lives. There's a lot of freedom in that notion.

Experience fear of falling

In this experience you will recall tendrils of spirit. I'm talking about the parts of you that feel secure because they are anchored around powerful experiences in your past. As long as you are tied to those weights, dragging them along, you will never be completely centred. There will always be energy leaching out of your present moment to feed the past, keeping it strong, putting where you've come from centre stage rather than fuelling who you are now.

20.1 a) **Visualisation:** Get yourself settled, get comfortable in your favourite meditating spot (I'm sure you've got one of those by this point in our partnership). Relax with some deep breathing.

Flow in and out with it. Feel the sensation breathing creates around your nostrils, the sound made as you inhale and exhale.

Just be here with yourself for a few minutes.

When you're ready, imagine yourself walking through a lovely garden.

The lawns stretch out in all directions. There are beds of flowers, bushes, shrubs, and broad canopied trees shading gorgeously wrought benches. There are water features, everything looks neat, and proper, and correct. This is your own private botanical gardens.

In the distance, there is a dense patch of darker green. There is a stone wall around that darker, distant part of the garden. The trees on the other side of the wall are wilder.

Make your way over there.

As you get closer you see how massive and gnarled the old tree trunks are. There is ivy climbing them, up into the dense canopy. There are crazy leaved bushes and plants overgrown and spilling over the top of the wall.

Find the door.

Push your way inside.

You know there is something at the centre of this wild garden waiting for you. It's important. You go with the tug of sensation that pulls you towards the centre, but as you move through the overgrown foliage, the plants snag at your clothes.

Each time you are caught up, look into the leaves of the plant that has you. You'll find a note, rolled into a scroll and tucked into the branches. Unroll the scroll. Written there is one word that represents something that is holding you back; this one word connects to an event in your past that you think defines you, and makes you who you are.

Chapter 20 ○ Resisting Change

You aren't looking for bad or good, negative or positive moments. Just powerful moments.

Accept the first instinct you receive—no second-guessing in the garden. Continue in this way: moving through the brush until you are snagged, collecting your note, tucking it into your pocket. It may happen once, or many times. Keep going until you reach the centre.

At the centre of the garden is your journal. Pick it up, tuck all the notes inside the front cover. Turn back and take the same path to the door in the stone wall. The path widens for you, there are no snags now.

Leave the garden and shut the door. You see there is a key in the lock now. Lock the door. Take the key and walk back to the centre of the grand, flowing lawn.

Come back to your body. Wiggle your bits. Blink yourself awake. Pick up your real-life journal and follow on with the next exercise.

Experience 108 Fear of Falling - Visualisation

20.1 b)   **Journalling:** Get a loose piece of paper and tear it into slips. Write down the words from the notes you collected in your wild garden, each word on its own slip of paper. Then, sit with each one. Write a story in your workbook about each connection.

Why this word?

Why is this moment powerful?

Why did it snag?

Why do you have to keep it tied securely to your spirit?

What would happen if it wasn't anchoring you?

_____
_____
_____
_____
_____ Continue →

Part IV · SPROUT

Chapter 20 — Resisting Change

Experience 109 Fear of Falling - Journalling

20.1 c) **Playing:** Preparation steps for this exercise:

Step 1. You'll want several balls of yarn in different colours for this exercise.

Step 2. Gather the tags you collected in this section's journalling exercise and tuck them into a pocket.

Step 3. Put a pair of scissors (or pruning shears) in another pocket; you'll thank me for this.

Attach each tag to its own thread. You might connect a certain tag with a specific colour; let yourself be drawn to what feels appropriate. Don't second-guess yourself, or attempt to reason your way out of the inspiration with thoughts like yellow fits with this situation better than red. There are layers of magic taking hold, just go with it.

Tie one end of each strand of yarn to a wrist; depending on how many tags you're playing with, you might attach threads to both your wrists. Let the skeins of yarn drag behind you on the floor. Walk around the room, tangling yarn around everything. Go nuts and walk around the whole house feeling the discomfort of every snag and tug.

Hell, if you hear a crash in the distance take it as an indication of how influential your energetic tangles and hang-ups might actually be. What if the damage was visible, audible, obvious in its need to be cleaned up ALL THE TIME?

Once you are good and tangled, cut each thread in a way that leaves a bracelet on your wrist. Cut each with intention. Use your journalling discoveries to form the basis of your intention for severing the weight of each anchor. Don't worry about trying to do it in any particular order; you don't have to remember which tag is hanging on which colour thread. Do you dare to gather all the threads up into a bunch and hack through the whole lot in one go?

Collect all the threads, lying loose on the floor, unweave and untangle where you must. Gather up the remnants of whatever smashed during your weaving. Throw it all away. No burying it or burning it, definitely no tucking it into a bag to get rid of later. Go and throw it in the outside bin. Now.

Chapter 20   Resisting Change

The pieces of coloured yarn encircling your wrists represent the ways these powerful moments in your life have shaped you. They are part of you. They are part of the foundation upon which you walk, no longer the weights dragging you backwards.

_____
_____
_____
_____
_____
_____
_____
_____
_____
_____

Experience 110 Fear of Falling - Playing

20.2 Change is Exhausting

There seems to be an enormous amount of effort required to instigate and deliver yourself to a place of change, let alone get to the other side. Isn't that the reason you don't begin immediately after the moment of inspiration? We clutch at discomfort, even though it restricts our movement, even though it suggests that the time for growth has arrived. We are sure doing the thing will be much more uncomfortable.

Isn't the greatest discomfort of all the uncertainty? You don't know what might happen. Terrifying.

Guess what? You don't have to know. Anyone who purports to know is trying to game the system, and life doesn't care about human machinations. Life just gets on with itself.

Transition is the tenderest point of change. Did you know that transition is the term used to describe a birthing mother at the point of full cervical dilation before the surges of arrival begin? Until transition, her body has been labouring to open, create space for the arrival of what is unknown. One needs to be more than open in order for transition to flow into change; there is more work to be done, more effort to spend, farther to fall. This is but the turning point.

There is no way to resist the impending change, and yet we try. We try until our emotions are shredded, our physical body is puffy with punishment and neglect, our spirits are tangled.

Resisting saps your energy and leaves you feeling weak, worn, frayed around the edges. Have you ever experienced the elation of a change that you've flowed with, embraced, jumped into, knowing there is no chance that a net will catch your fall?

Compare the two experiences. Why does resistance remain an option? Fear of the unknown? That is a phrase often thrown around when someone is stuck in a loop, sinking in stagnancy. You know what I reckon? I think we are afraid of what we think we do know.

None of us know. Precognition is a window with a different view each time you open the blinds. There is a secret arrogance we walk around with. It is the voice that continually whispers, fuels our desire to stay safe. Its never-ending goal is to assure us that by standing still we have a measure of control over the general operating system of the universe. "Change is dangerous," murmurs the voice.

We must slip over the edge into unknown. The final part of this flowing with change thing is the release. It's not done, not truly meant, the spell is not over, until you throw your intention out into the universe and let the scattered pieces of yourself settle back to earth. Some of the pieces will blow away, they are empty husks and it is proper that they don't return. Could it be that the full-to-the-brim purpose that bloats your being is actually a collection of empty husks, clutched to your belly and stuffed down inside until their emptiness filled you up?

Experience change is exhausting

Time to lovingly shake our heads in exasperation and practise falling. Let's explore what you think you know.

20.2 a) **Visualisation:** Begin with normal, relaxed breathing—no forcing anything, or trying to relax your breath. Just observe it flowing in, flowing out.

Imagine your belly is a container for all the change that's taken place in your life. Each change is represented by a tiny mote.

Chapter 20 — Resisting Change

Your belly is filled with pinpoints of change. Some of them are sparkling and bright, some of them are the dusky dark of poppy seeds. Some are husks.

Do the pinpoints swirl like stars in the night sky, mixed into a whirlpool? Or is it still, there, in your belly?

Deepen your breaths. Imagine each breath flows down further into your body. Your practice is to gradually, one inhalation at a time, move your breath through the container of motes.

Work your way into your low belly, then into your pelvis, then into your thighs, where your breath will pour down your legs and into the earth.

What happens to the change motes? Do they swirl? Are they clumped, like dry mud? If they swirl, are you reminded of a dust devil, or a sparkling galaxy? There is no right or wrong here, just what is.

Breathe and observe. You don't need to fix anything. You aren't broken.

Experience 111 Change is Exhausting - Visualisation

20.2 b) **Deepening:** Let's stir things up. Ask the contents of the container in your belly what it needs to loosen up and allow your breath clear passage through the motes of change.

This is your personal visualisation and will depend on what you experienced in the last exercise. This is a chance for you to take your experience deeper. This is the moment you might deepen, sink, know yourself more intimately. This is a conversation with your instinctual mind, your gut-mind.

Put your hands over your belly. Feel the warmth of the connection with the skin of your palms.

If it feels right, stir your hands over your belly in a clockwise motion. Make your touch gentle, caressing, caring, loving. Can you do that?

Breathe with the release, the flow, the shifting energy in your belly. Allow the motes to fly up, fall down. Use your breath to support their movement.

End this exercise by grounding your breath through your legs, out the soles of your feet, and into the earth.

Experience 112 Change is Exhausting - Deepening

20.2 c) **Journalling:** Sweetheart, sometimes change is hard. Sometimes it hurts. Sometimes you think it is going to hurt too much and so you feel tired before you begin.

Here is a secret: you have already begun. It's your resistance to what is happening that's making you feel so weary. Capture your weariness with some journalling.

What are you tired of?

_____

_____

_____

_____

_____

Chapter 20 — Resisting Change

Experience 113 Change is Exhausting - Journalling

20.2 d) **Release:** It's time to get your fingers in the dirt. There is even a chance of getting dirt in your hair with this one. This exercise is so simple, and deeply connected to the practice in this section.

Take everything, every idea, notion, feeling, shift, half breathed breath, word that you've stirred up in this section and go outside. Find a patch of dirt, bucket of sand, pile of grass clippings, heap of leaves.

Get your hands full of your chosen elemental partner and hold it lovingly. Form an intention: imbue the material in your hold with the power of release.

Close your eyes and tip your head back, take a breath and toss. Know that as the material scatters, the grains of dirt and blades of grass carry with them those motes of change from your belly that are ready to release.

This is change in motion, your energy in action. This is you practising elemental magic for emotional healing.

Experience 114 Change is Exhausting - Release

20.3 God Goddess All That Is

Typing that heading, I hear my mother's voice. *God Goddess All That Is*. I used to let the words pass by, trying my best to get the end of the phrase without actually hearing any of them. The me that hears the words is still sixteen years old and clueless.

Clueless and certain—that's a magical combination to fuel true adventure. It's only now I begin to appreciate the subtle tastes of the delicious folly I am. But we all are that kind of folly. I wouldn't wish to be any other way; it tells me I'm growing and alive. It tells me I hold my younger self with compassion and respect. I'm learning to appreciate the flavours of change. It's a feast that I've mostly nibbled, sometimes mindlessly gobbled, and, in later years, bitten my tongue off rather than taste at all.

Seriously, I actually have nerve damage in my jaw that severs feeling to the left side of my tongue. No taste. No feeling. I can take a chunk out of myself and not realise until the damage is done. Pain is confused with pressure and pressure tickles. The whole healing journey around this particular injury is worth its own book. I'll add it to the list of stories to be written.

I sit here in my forty-five year old body and let my eyes scan across the words. *God Goddess All That Is*. I can soften my understanding, lean back and relax, lean in and allow the sensation to envelop me. There is an all-ness to the phrase that eluded me back then. How could it have been any other way? I could not have known then what I know now. I have been several different people between then and now. We all know what we know when we know it, and not a moment before.

God Goddess All That Is is one of those phrases that attempts to capture the essence of eternity. One might just as easily say one's own name and understand that it holds the same immense experience of connection and understanding. What do you think about that, lovely one?

Experience God Goddess All That Is

There is a balance in life of which you are a part. You are neither entirely one thing nor the other. If you were to sit on the bar of the scales of life you would be constantly sliding from one side to the other, in active motion, all the time. This section of experience opens appreciation of wherever it is you are now.

20.3 a)   **Active meditation:** Today, every time you eat something, drink something, really taste what you are putting into your mouth. Pause to chew, feel the texture against the roof of your mouth, breathe with gratitude. This is fuel for life.

Experience 115 God Goddess All That Is - Active Meditation

20.3 b)   **Contemplation:** Take your smartphone and open the voice memo app. Record your name in your own voice five times, with several seconds silence between each vocalisation.

What form of your name did you choose to record? If you are practising this experience for the second (or third, or fourth) time, what has changed, why has it changed?

Centre yourself, get settled—you know how that goes now. Press play on your device. Press play as many times as you want to. Then press it once more, when you don't want to.

_____
_____
_____
_____
_____
_____
_____
_____
_____
_____

Experience 116 God Goddess All That Is - Contemplation

20.3 c)   **Journalling:** Define your idea of perfection.

Write the words, "Sondra says I'm perfect, right now, just as I am."

1. Write a letter to me, telling me why I'm wrong.

Chapter 20 — Resisting Change

2. Now, write me a letter telling me why I'm right.

Continue →

Part IV SPROUT

Send a copy of letter 2 to my private email address: sondra@goddesskindled.com and prove me right. What a gift, to be granted the opportunity to connect with your vulnerable self and celebrate your experience of embodying earth. Thank you, sweetheart.

Experience 117 God Goddess All That Is - Journalling

21

FINDING BALANCE

21.1 Fear and Anger

This section is one I feel far from qualified to write. Though, they say teaching a thing is the best way to learn it. Shall we muddle through this together, then? That's not to say I don't have experience with fear or anger. The stories I could tell… Probably do tell in themes and metaphors scattered through all my writing.

Probably? Without doubt.

I call myself unqualified to address especially anger, because my habit has been to not address it at all. My conditioning was such that the merest whiff of angry expression by someone was enough to trigger a system-wide shut down in me. It's like a universal hand would flick one giant finger and unplug me from source.

I'm changing.

These days, I try to yank the plug from the socket myself; sometimes I succeed, but I feel empty rather than protected by the action. There is no comfort or soothing distance created, no buffer, no shield, no safety.

Four days ago, I didn't even attempt to unplug. I turned towards my anger. I was indignant, pissed off, affronted, offended.

I questioned my anger. In most cases I burrow my way through it to fear. In every case, my fear turns out to be uncertainty of what might happen if I let my anger show. Then I come back to the beginning of the question and ask again, "Why?" This instance was no different.

The final question that always pushes up through my righteous indignation is this: Why do you need to be right? If I have the courage to grab onto this root and let it pull me beneath, into the underworld of Self, I can discover the wound that calls to be loved.

Part IV ⟡ SPROUT

I might go beneath. I could—but for the fear of finding what lies there. Anger and fear are so intimately intertwined; it is only with effort that I can loosen the knots enough to see the connections. If I dare to peer, lean in, get nose-to-knot, I lose the connection and know they are the same thread. Beginning and end are not important; they have fused and become one. No. They always were the same, different only by being seen through my filter of the moment, my triggered reaction to what would have been an utterly benign happening for someone else.

Let's call this our anger into fear into anger feedback loop. I'll add an extra 'into fear' in there, since that's usually where I end up before pulling out.

I do not claim to have finished with this one; the wound is still open and calling for attention. The bleeding is deep. There are layers of weeping scab that just didn't do the trick, didn't seal, got infected and repellent; disgusting is easy to turn away from.

But, I keep returning.

This spiral is teaching me how to hold personal boundaries—something that doesn't come easily, hence each return, and the deepening nature of this pattern. This is not a flat spiral. It is a spring that stretches down into the centre of my gut-mind, the place of instinct and knowing.

By consistently questioning these triggering moments I grow, love myself, accept each feeling, and let it flow through. I don't have to unplug any more. I don't have to be right, but I remain insatiably curious about why I want to be right. I think it's a power thing. It's a power thing because the people to whom we ordinarily grant authority are the ones we believe are right.

Seldom do we give that authority to ourselves—we crave it though. I want that power: to be on the side of the dynamic I perceive as the active one, the strong partner. I've used fear and the act of playing the victim with terrific success over the course of my life.

Poor me.

Take care of me.

See how worthy I am of your care.

Feed your power back to me through this hook that I ever so gently slide into your heart.

Finding balance is the way through this puzzle. Changing sides of the dynamic only takes us to another position of imbalance. It's a case of sliding through centre, dipping into each side in turn, and then carrying that wisdom back through centre—and, repeat.

Chapter 21 Finding Balance

Experience fear and anger

Touching anger is difficult for those of us who have never learned healthy ways to experience this awesome emotion. I'm learning how to sit with anger. I'm learning how to love the fear that it triggers within me. In order to explore the existing connections we have, expand our ideas and beliefs, the first thing to do is locate the relevant emotion. We need to lean into the fear, the trepidation, the shadow. Let's do this together, and practise channelling the emotions for growth and empowerment.

21.1 a) **Active meditation:** Time to open your ground. Head outside. Your backyard is great, if you have one. If you don't have a backyard, do you have a balcony? If you don't have a balcony, do you have a pot plant? Go somewhere you can dig in the dirt.

As you worm your fingertips into the soil, imagine you are searching for the thing that makes you angry. Yes! That one! Right then, you thought of something: a situation, conversation, moment, event. Don't pretend you didn't. That's the one you are digging for, right now.

It might take a few repetitions of this exercise to get your fingertips into the moment. It might take several times to get your hands completely coated in the connection. This is deep work, lovely. Take your time. Don't force yourself. Be kind. You can do this.

When you think you have achieved connection, come back another time and do this exercise again. Anger is wily, and not only for those of us who are confrontation averse. It's seductive, practised at making you think you have seen its real face.

Keep coming back until you can locate the connection in your body; you will know when this happens because there will be uncertainty and sadness at the edges. Your anger will feel unexpectedly welcoming. Your heart will thump and tell you it's time to deal.

_____
_____
_____
_____
_____ Continue →

Experience 118 Fear and Anger - Active Meditation

21.1 b) **Journalling:** After each time you dig your fingers in search of anger, take the time to reflect in your journal. This is the sifting of the dirt you've brought to light and carried inside your home beneath your fingernails.

This is where the small pebbles that have hidden in your shoes for years, hobbling you at inappropriate moments, are revealed. Tears? Beautiful. They add soul juice to the dirt and make muddy streaks through your words.

Let your words spill across the page until you realise that there have never been any inappropriate moments.

Chapter 21 ⟲ Finding Balance

(lined journaling space)

Experience 119 Fear and Anger - Journalling

21.1 c)   **Deepening:** How willing are you to be powerful? How willing you are is in direct proportion to how much responsibility you are willing to shoulder. The responsibility for your actions, what you do in response to feeling a feeling about a thought that pops into your consciousness, is entirely yours. You are the only one who can direct what happens, regardless of what you are currently telling yourself.

Part IV ꧁ SPROUT

Unless you can own your own shit, power is not yours. Practise squishing the stink between your toes, burrow your feet into it, let it nourish your growth.

Take some small pieces of paper. Write one keyword on each that connects you to an aspect of the thing that made you angry, the thing you were digging for.

Go to the place you've been digging for anger. Make a mud puddle.

Add the revelations of your journalling to the muck: plant the keywords.

Get barefooted and step into the mud. Now squelch, squirm, wriggle, stomp. If a few tears fall into the mix, so much the better. Nourish your soul. Take it all in, feel all the sensations—on your skin and inside your body.

_____
_____
_____
_____
_____
_____

Experience 120 Fear and Anger - Deepening

PART V

UNFURL

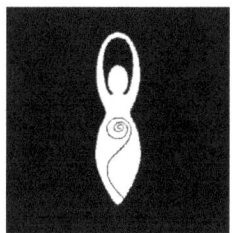

"Life shrinks or expands in proportion to one's courage."
—Anaïs Nin

22

COURAGEOUS BEGINNINGS

22.1 Breathing Into the Quote

Following is the quote and meditation that frames this part.

"Life shrinks or expands in proportion to one's courage." –Anaïs Nin

What is courage? More than that, what is courage for you? More than that, what is courage for you today? The answers to these questions will change, flowing with your mood, your robustness or fragility, your life.

Fragility is not the antithesis of courage. There is enormous strength and power in the softest parts of your heart. In fact, right at the centre of the most unguarded part of your spirit is where you will discover a sense of courage more resilient and timeless than you thought possible.

It is when we come to the end of the line, the last step, the final fraying thread to which we cling as the abyss yawns wide beneath us, that we release into that softest of places inside. We may as well, since this is it. What's left to lose?

Everything. Thank Goddess, everything.

Experience the proportion of your courage

Welcome to your abyss, darling.

22.1 a) **Contemplation:** Sit with the words of this section's quote. Take the time to feel all the ways it makes you feel. Journal your contemplation.

_____ Continue →

Part V UNFURL

_____
_____
_____
_____
_____
_____
_____
_____
_____
_____

Answer the questions posed in the paragraph following the quote:

What is courage?

_____
_____
_____
_____
_____

What is courage for you?

_____
_____
_____
_____
_____
_____

Chapter 22 ⚲ Courageous Beginnings

What is courage for you today?

_____
_____
_____
_____
_____
_____

Experience 121 The Proportion of Your Courage - Contemplation

22.1 b) **Making magic:** Do one courageous thing. Read your definition of courage, and apply it to one moment of your day today.

Relax your thinking about what courage should look like, and do the action, think the thought, release that rule (which is someone else's, anyway), allow your self-kindness to swell and be the container for your courage.

Experience 122 The Proportion of Your Courage - Making Magic

22.1 c) **Ritual:** Document the one courageous thing you did. Lay it out on paper, write down the thoughts you thought, the symbolism you included, the steps you took.

_____
_____
_____
_____
_____
_____
_____
_____ Continue →

Part V 🌀 UNFURL

_____
_____
_____
_____
_____

How might you apply this framework to other moments in your life that require courageous action?

_____
_____
_____
_____
_____
_____
_____
_____
_____
_____
_____
_____
_____
_____

This is magic, this is spellwork, this is powerful ritual; claim it.

Experience 123 The Proportion of Your Courage - Ritual

23

READY TO RECEIVE

23.1 Seeing Your Life

The courage to expand my life has been a powerful force of late. Of late—how literary of me. Lately, I've been giving my body permission to tell me what it wants. Apparently, what it wants is to be heard, and it wants to scream at me for a while before we settle into anything resembling polite conversation. I wonder if our interactions will ever be polite. I've treated my body as an entity without agency for so long; it's going to take a while to get her to trust me.

I need help.

For the first time I can remember, those three little words, I need help, feel powerful, expansive. Vulnerable—yes—but in a way that feels rooted into the deep black richness of dirt that is fecund, just waiting for my intention to writhe into it and shift the grains. I'm making space for myself within a supported environment. I'm reaching through what I know and opening myself up to another healer's hands.

One of the filters I see my life through is one that goes a little something like this:

"I am a healer, a therapist, I know this stuff. I should be able to heal myself. If I can't heal myself, how can I possibly put myself out there and ask clients to trust me to help them heal?"

Do you see how I limit myself with this belief?

The whole point of someone coming to spend time with me in healing space is for me to hold them, to offer a shifted perspective, to prompt, to hear, to witness, to ground.

Part V ⸻ UNFURL

I never "heal" anyone. I hold space in which they can heal themselves. I have known this, said this, from the first moment I knowingly invited clients into my tiny private clinic in the downstairs room of my house, about a thousand years ago. I think I've been doing it for lifetimes; I'm fairly certain I've been killed at least twice for being an outspoken, fierce, powerful healer. They are a whole other magical reality, stories for other times.

It's true, of course—I can't be this same person for myself! It's not possible, not in the same way.

Today, I sent an email to someone I hope will be my yoga teacher. I've never had a healing relationship with a yoga teacher, having made it a habit to ignore my physical body's requests for nourishment. The blockages I've worked through so far, for this specific instance, are:

- You won't understand what's going on, your Dutch isn't good enough (I'm an Aussie, living in the Netherlands).
- Your hip and spine are too weak and painful.
- You're going to look stupid because you don't understand what everyone is saying.
- You're only going to give up after a few sessions, why start?
- It's too expensive.

None of these statements is real. They are all imagined assumptions designed to keep me shut up inside my house, and mind, and body. The relationship I have with me seems to occasionally smack of abuse. How is your relationship with you?

Experience seeing your life

Where did your patterns of behaviour come from? Does it even matter? In this moment, what is true? Patterns are projections from our unconscious in the absence of immediate presence in this moment. Clearing away, piercing the filters, allowing fresh air and new dawn light in is a great place to begin. It is in these moments we see anew, we see true. This is when we are ready to receive, and we transform into the teacher that appears in the space we have opened.

23.1 a) **Journalling:** Your writing prompt is, "I am …" Begin every sentence with those two words and write until you lose yourself. Consider this: you're actually finding yourself.

_____

_____

Chapter 23 — Ready to Receive

_____
_____
_____
_____
_____
_____
_____
_____
_____
_____
_____
_____
_____
_____
_____
_____
_____
_____
_____
_____
_____
_____

Experience 124 Seeing Your Life - Journalling

23.1 b) **Contemplation:** Go for a walk. Stop when you are pulled to notice a tree, a plant, stretch of lawn, a patch of green. Perhaps you have a favourite regular walk through a local park or wooded area, and you know exactly which tree is calling to you as you read this.

When you get there, sit down in a place from which you can pour all your attention towards the tree, or bit of green, that is your focus.

Loosen your rules of what it is you're looking at. Be a child, with eyes that have never seen this thing. See everything, name nothing. There are no rules about how to categorise this thing upon which you contemplate. Lose yourself in what you observe.

___

Experience 125 Seeing Your Life - Contemplation

23.1 c) **Deepening:** Settle in, somewhere lush and comfy. You are the focus this time. Apply the same contemplation to yourself, as you did to the green in the last exercise.

Untie the threads that keep in place all your rules about what you are. Have you ever seen a baby discovering her hands, her toes, her voice, her laugh? Be that innocent, that insatiably curious about what you are.

Close your eyes and go within, with the same sense of wonder and curiosity.

(writing lines)

Experience 126 Seeing Your Life - Deepening

23.2 THE MUCKY STUFF

There is a tendency for cleanliness in modern life that leaves little room for Goddessliness. Clean skin, smooth skin; no hair—down there, under here, below the knees. Why is his hair manly, and mine not womanly? Fuck that. My hair is humanly, Goddessly, naturally, rebelliously, here to stay. Take this rant inside, into the invisible world of your mind. Drag it up to the locked door of your wild heart and slam it against the ancient wood until it splinters.

How often do you tidy up your thoughts before putting them into words, before admitting them to yourself, for that matter? I'm not talking about negative, or positive, being necessary, being kind, or generous. This has nothing to do with kindness. Scratch that, this is all about self-kindness—the lack of it.

Let me introduce you to a category of unkindness that we constantly mislabel as impropriety. Each occurrence is another delicate net of dry moss, another sharp twig, all layered between the multitude of tiny embers you think you've damped down far enough to extinguish.

That's not ladylike.

Don't rock the boat.

Close your legs.

Wear that, and you're asking for it.

Mind your manners.

Are you feeling the stirring of a scream somewhere around your belly button, about now? I am. Make no mistake, that feeling you're having—it's rage, the sort that smoulders. How does that statement sit with you? As opposed to outrage, which does have an active component, what you're feeling is more likely inrage.

I'm speaking of an ongoing attack on the most intimate parts of my psyche. Inrage is automatic behaviour and has been part of my makeup for as far back as I can recall. It's the way I stay safe, keep the peace, don't rock the boat, be invisible. I wonder if you also have your own term for the act of soul desecration? Healthy expression of anger was never part of my education. I'm still softening into the possibility that rage could be a loving support in my healing and growth.

There's profound self-harm contained in inrage. Perhaps my act of inventing a word to encapsulate a lifetime of inwardly-directed criticism signals my willingness to enter into the dance of exploration and understanding. Criticism is a sanitised phrase in this instance. Let me be explicit with what is going unsaid: shame, disgust, hate, abhorrence. And all these destructive energies, which is what these emotions are, swirl through your body triggering chemical combinations that eventually lash your physical systems to shreds. Think of it as internal self-flagellation. Its only purpose is to tell lies, keep you focused on ensuring the smouldering wreckage of your spirit doesn't ignite. You must, after all, keep everyone else safe; there is a monster inside you.

Inrage is the experience of swallowing all the mucky stuff, because it's too dirty for anyone to see. But you did see, whether you acknowledge it or not. You did feel. One day, your howl will sound; you'll be ready to peel back the numbness and plunge your hand into the muck; you'll stir it around, lift out your paw, admire your claws dripping with molten pain. One day, soon, you'll paint the walls with it.

Experience the mucky stuff

Time to shift your inrage to that beautiful, helpful, active place of enrage. Once you're enraged, you can do something with it.

Chapter 23 — Ready to Receive

23.2 a) **Journalling:** Choose one of the catalytic statements above as your writing prompt. I'll give them to you again here, to keep your smouldering sooty red:

That's not ladylike.

Don't rock the boat.

Close your legs.

Wear that, and you're asking for it.

Mind your manners.

Write a statement on the next journalling line. Set your pen to the paper and let your words splatter all over the clean space. Remember, nobody is looking over your shoulder. Shock your inner critic: be wild, profane, gloriously abandoned. Journal into your mucky stuff.

_____

_____

_____

_____

_____

_____

_____

_____

_____

_____

_____

_____

_____

_____

_____

_____

Part V ⟡ UNFURL

Experience 127 The Mucky Stuff - Journalling

23.2 b) **Release:** Get the largest canvas you can find: one of those seemingly endless rolls of butcher paper from a craft shop, an old shower curtain, an actual canvas—as wide as your arms can reach, a discarded wooden panel from that ancient stash under your house.

Gather some tubes of paint.

Dress yourself for ritual; you're going to get messy with this one.

Set up your canvas: on the back lawn (hell, on the front lawn!), nailed to the fence, propped on an easel atop a big-arse drop cloth—trust me; you're going to need the drop cloth.

Take the lids of your paints of choice, and lay them out so each one is easy to pick up. Open one hand, gaze into your palm; sink into the centre, bleed out along all the lines, trace your fingertips.

Select your first colour and squeeze a snake of paint onto your hand, next colour, next, and the next; fill the cup of your hand with paint.

Gaze into your palm again. Sink, and bleed, and flow into all the colours.

Close your hand. Feel the slick colours slide between your fingers; let your awareness slip into all the tender gaps with the moist mess.

Now, flick the paint onto the canvas.

Repeat.

Great Goddess, repeat until you feel the release of roaring.

Chapter 23 Ready to Receive

_____
_____
_____
_____

Experience 128 The Mucky Stuff - Release

23.2 c) **Cleansing:** This exercise naturally flows on from the previous one. Wipe your painted hands over the clothes that cover your thighs, your belly, your breasts, your arse.

Replace the lids on the tubes of paint—those that have any contents remaining. Leave everything where it is.

You're in the backyard and it's starting to rain? Too perfect for words. It's a mess and the kids are due home from school in an hour? Fantastic. Here is the fuel for a bedtime story.

Strip off your clothes and leave them with your canvas and paint.

Get into the shower. Stand under the water and watch the colours bleed into each other and spiral down the drain.

Know that there is magic remaining on your skin, in your touch, splattered inside your thoughts.

Wash yourself with the love and gentle care you would reserve for a newborn; such you are.

_____
_____
_____
_____
_____
_____

Experience 129 The Mucky Stuff - Cleansing

24

THE WEIGHT OF WHITE

24.1 Overwhelm

White is perfection. It's unmarred by any mistake, any misstep. And, depending upon which mood I'm in, or which pattern is active in my subconscious, it can be inviting, or a dire warning to keep away!

There's a universal rule that activates whenever I don a white shirt. You know which rule I'm talking about. It's the rule that triggers the same day that spaghetti, rich red wine casserole, or curry is on the menu. The fact that I'm the cook in our house and select every menu is beside the point. Splat, right on the generous top curve of one of my boobs. Some days it screams of attention seeking, some days it's just a tiny tear of red wine, cried by accident.

White is the colour of death; it's the colour of baby's breath. It's virginal (apparently). Maidenhood is draped in white, and you might mistake a true maiden for some wispy, helpless, untouched creature. But she, like white, is surrounded by contradiction in symbolism. After all, pure and virginal are not equivalent aspects of life; neither are maiden and sensual exclusive states of being.

For me, the demand for perfection is the shadow existence of white. Not unexpected, then, is the triggering of emotional numbness in those of us for whom perfection is the constant scream in the back of our mind. Perfection is, of course, an illusion. It's a trick of the mind it hides behind. Perfection stays invisible, even while it shreds our willingness to try with shrieking.

What the fuck does perfection even look like? Whose is the face, action, expectation that sparked your illusion of perfection?

I'm going to take a few moments to swear a bit more. My office has a really high ceiling: great acoustics. Maybe I can antagonise the ones who embody my ideas of perfection enough they materialise. Maybe we finally lose ourselves in this *dans macabre*. Maybe today I have enough heat to thaw the numbness. But it's okay if my heat is not up to the task. Becoming aware, not running away, sitting with the numbness, they are all worthy healing medicines.

You get to define the magic of your comfort zone. You get to decide what is safe today. Don't punish yourself for not feeling, for not immediately registering the slice of cruel words, the dull thud of dismissal, the vague look through you that makes you wonder if your words made it past your lips, or the person is just wondering what the hell you are doing there.

There are two things that emotional numbness does: it tethers you completely inside the moment, and it blasts everything away in order for you to completely deny the moment. Contradictions.

Experience overwhelm

You'll have to do some prep for this experience, but I promise it will be worth it. You are going to get messy (again), but, another promise, you're going to love it in the end. If you don't love it the first time, if it feels like you're breaking rules and must not—perfect!

24.1 a)   **Sensing:** Find a white shirt. If it's new, so much the better. In fact, go pick up a pack of inexpensive t-shirts, or tank tops, or button-up shirts with collars. You'll want to do this exercise more than once.

Buy some fruit. Make it something juicy, like watermelon, mango, or oranges.

Now, get messy. Use your hands to pull the fruit apart. Bite into the flesh with your teeth. Cut a big slice and take a chomp too big to fit into your mouth.

Do not wipe any drips off your chin. Keep eating. Taste every morsel of flavour. Experience every tickle of juice as it trails over your forearms, down your neck.

The next exercise follows on from this one.

Experience 130 Overwhelm - Sensing

24.1 b)   **Deepening:** Take off your shirt. <u>Do not</u> wipe your face. Use your shirt to mop up any juice that's been dripped over the furniture, over the floor, over the plate, over your legs, between your toes, in the crease of your armpit. (You might need to get a mop or wet cloth later, but hey—this is soulwork! Sticky bits are guaranteed.)

Pay attention to your actions. Be completely present with your mess. Now, go get into the shower and let the water run over your body, your face, the way the juice did.

Take your shirt in with you. Put it on the floor of the shower and use your toes to massage the juice from its fabric.

Experience 131 Overwhelm - Deepening

24.1 c) **Journalling:** Write about this experience. Pay particular attention to how you felt when you had to mop up the spilled juice with your shirt, and the reaction you had to my instruction to NOT wipe your face.

_____
_____
_____
_____
_____
_____
_____
_____
_____
_____
_____
_____
_____
_____
_____
_____
_____
_____

Part V UNFURL

Did you clean up all the stray drips with a wet cloth, mop the floor, before you headed for your journal? Write about that, too.

Chapter 24 ♉ The Weight of White

_____

_____

_____

_____

_____

_____

_____

_____

_____

_____

_____

_____

_____

Experience 132 Overwhelm - Journalling

3.2 THE SAFETY OF THE WILD

The tug of war between staying safe and stepping into the wilder nature of one's self pretends to be a delicate balancing act. But there's nothing delicate about it. There is a call that echoes in the back of your gut calling you back to the power of your wildness.

Wildness doesn't mean out of control. There is profound sacredness in mud, and muck, and shit.

Too much emphasis on the pristine parts of your existence pulls you out of balance and into the smothering place, where you imagine breathing too loudly draws unwanted attention. The place from where, if you don't tear yourself away, you both fear you will cease to be, and hope you will pop out of existence.

Sudden ripping away towards our wild nature seems more sudden to people looking on than the person pulling herself free. The freeing has been going on for much longer than is apparent to any observer, no matter how close the relationship. Always, the relationship you have with Self is more intimate.

Tell me what is safer: clean obedience, where everything is taken care of for you, you are provided for and loved (really?) so long as you don't rock the boat; or the dirty unknown, opening the door to weird things, risking being misunderstood to seek answers to questions you dare not ask.

You've been wondering *what would happen if…* longer than anyone realises.

When the final shove comes you might pretend it is unwelcome, but you and I know better. There is a sigh of relief disguised in your grunt of surprise.

If you were to really investigate all the moments you felt trapped, or constrained, the years of inane doings that had no purpose other than a daily grind to keep up appearances, what would you truly discover? The consistent part of all those moments is you.

Experience the safety of the wild

It's time to buy your bible. Get a copy of *Women Who Run With the Wolves*, by Dr. Clarissa Pinkola Estés. Don't start reading it, yet. Put it on your altar for a while; let's explore and explode your actions, intentions, and reactions to this instruction.

24.2 a) **Journalling:** Write about all the ways my instructions, above, make you feel.

What does the word "bible" trigger in your imagination, in your body?

What does the word "altar" trigger in your imagination, in your body?

_____
_____
_____
_____
_____
_____
_____
_____
_____
_____

Chapter 24 — The Weight of White

Experience 133 The Safety of the Wild - Journalling

24.2 b) **Ritual:** If you have an altar, when was the last time you gave it attention?

If you think you don't have an altar, think again. Which is the table, tucked out of the way, where you place objects sacred to you? Which is the centrepiece you change as the seasons change? Which is the candle you regularly light simply because it pleases you to do so?

Give your altar some love. Freshen its energy. Sweep away the dust and old patterns; remove anything that is only there because you force yourself to keep it, because it should be important to you (except it really isn't).

Experience 134 The Safety of the Wild - Ritual

24.2 c) **Spellwork:** You are going to prepare a wilding potion. You will need: a small, clean jar with a lid, clean dirt, water, sandalwood or jasmine essential oil.

Lay out all the ingredients on your altar. Combine dirt and water in the jar to make a thick mud potion. Add a few drops of essential oil.

Mix the potion with a finger. While you stir, think about why you want to read the book on your altar. What knowledge do you hope to find, wisdom do you long for?

Press a fingerprint to the inside of the front cover of your book.

Experience 135 The Safety of the Wild - Spellwork

24.2 d) **Deepening:** Before getting into bed, go to your altar, open your wilding potion, and give it a stir. With your stirring finger, press a dot of mud just above your eyebrows, in the centre of your forehead.

When you wash the excess off your hands, know that these grains of earth are flowing back to earth, connecting you to the Great Mother, who holds you safely no matter how far your dreams take you.

Take your book to bed with you. Read a chapter, section, page, paragraph, sentence. Sink into every word. Spend time with the text. Allow the spaces between the words to be as meaningful as the words themselves.

When you have read your fill, press your finger to the potion print inside the front cover and set the book aside. Sleep.

Write about your dreams the next day; or don't. This is your magic. Your choice. Know that, as you sleep, you are healing on deep psychological and spiritual levels.

_____
_____
_____
_____
_____

Chapter 24 — The Weight of White

Experience 136 The Safety of the Wild - Deepening

25

QUICKENING

25.1 Outrunning Belligerence

There is an overwhelming surge of power generated in the act of tearing away from a stagnant state of being. Often it manifests as belligerence. It's such a delicious sensation; the invitation to hurl caution out the window is irresistible.

You regurgitate all the silent fuck yous that you've swallowed over the years. They fill your chest with their potentised howl—and you do howl. Let it shred the remaining mask of your old identity with the force of the eruption. The result is naked vulnerability.

Your flesh has been sandblasted. You are transitioning, and this is the slice of time immediately after one cycle ends, and before the next picks up momentum.

It's a cycle all of its own and cannot be skipped. These are seconds, hours, days, weeks to be treasured. *You* are to be treasured. It's going to be difficult to hold it all together. The trick is not to try. Fall apart completely. Please?

You've awoken, and there is no going back.

All the times you were gaslighted by your significant other, your boss, some random acquaintance visit your memory. All the insecurity is smacked awake; this is a testing time. It is not possible to run far or fast enough to outrun the need to shake free from the final hooks that still snag your spirit.

They will drag along the ground behind you, a skeleton, blasted apart and tied in fragmented terror to your ankles. The decayed remains of the existence you've torn away from. The bones are strong, and that's brilliant, because that is where the magic is stored.

Stop running.

Gather all your bones.

You don't have to know how to reassemble them into their former shape; they no longer need to be connected. Each is its own part of your story. Thread them together in whatever form pleases you best.

Hang the bone forms from trees, tangle them together, scatter them among the fallen branches of your psyche. Salt and burn them if you must. Eventually, you will be ready to sit in gratitude for every moment that forged them.

It's okay if that time is not quite yet, lovely one.

Experience outrunning belligerence

This experience will deepen your understanding of why you are the way you are. It will open you up to self-reflection and the chance to forgive. It's deep stuff, and will be an ongoing exercise that takes years to complete. That's normal. That's living, and growing.

25.1 a) **Journalling:** Who is the person you are sure you will never be able to forgive? Who is it that you don't have any desire to let off the hook? Are there more than one? That's okay, just select one for each time you do this exercise, and really delve into why you feel the way you do. Be as raw and naked in your writing as you can bring yourself to be.

_____
_____
_____
_____
_____
_____
_____
_____
_____
_____
_____
_____

Chapter 25 Quickening

Experience 137 Outrunning Belligerence - Journalling

Part V UNFURL

25.1 b)   **Deepening:** Go hunting. You are hunting for a collection of things you can scatter.

These scatterable pieces represent your bones. Each one symbolises a hook still quivering in your flesh.

Here are some suggestions: toothpicks, spent matches, twigs, plastic chopsticks, small bones. I add the option of bones into the list, because they are things I actually have around the house. To be more precise, my girlfriend, the shaman, has bones all over the place. But, as I've said on previous occasions, that's another story.

You're going to scatter them.

Finding one will act as a trigger for one of your hooks to come to mind. When it does, you have the opportunity to do something with your symbolic bone.

The intention is that you'll find them again over a long time, beneath the furniture, stuck in the underside of cushions, wedged into a crack between floorboards. So, make sure you take your living arrangements into consideration. You don't want to be scattering toothpicks about if you have a crawling baby or other small mammals living with you. The chopstick or twig options are probably the ones to go for in your case.

Each time you find one, I want you to give it your full attention.

Consider the following:

Are you ready to chuck it out?

Has it transformed into something softer, which begs to be tied into wind chimes and hung in the open?

Does it need to be hurled back over your shoulder to settle somewhere else and await discovery another time?

_____

_____

_____

_____

Chapter 25 Quickening

_____
_____
_____
_____

Experience 138 Outrunning Belligerence - Deepening

25.2 Protective Instincts

No, you aren't going mad. You aren't crazy, or deluded, or mistaken, or any of the other things people have tried to convince you of over the years. Your feelings are valid, and terribly powerful. They charge you up, and can feel as though they deplete you in the same instant. I imagine it's a lot like being struck by lightning.

Protection is about opening as fully as possible in the face of charging overwhelm.

Yes, I mean that. It does sound counterintuitive. I know it does. It continues to feel counterintuitive when we first begin to consciously practise this way of being.

There remains an element of danger that keeps our faces pressed to the glass, awaiting the next flash of power. This alertness is the trigger to open to the possibility that you actually know exactly what you are about.

You are so powerful that any lightning strike, rather than blowing you apart, highlights the next brilliance of your being that is calling for your attention. You are so grounded that the energy runs freely through your body, and unimpeded into the earth. It's blockage that causes destruction and distress, not the unexpected bolt from the blue.

Have you ever heard the term "beginner mind"? Whenever I remind you to remain curious, this is the state of mind to which I'm referring. It's all of those free-flowing metaphors that symbolise a stream, free of debris. But it's more than that. Curiosity is what takes us by the hand and leads us beneath what is immediately apparent. Beginner mind is having no opinion, no need to be right.

It's never time for making your mind up, regardless of what Bucks Fizz says. Go on and google that if you need a moment of lightness. Cultivating a robust sense of the ridiculous is one of the wisest practices you can develop.

Appreciate ridiculousness without condescension or judgement, with the enjoyment of a child who doesn't need to make the other person less than to enjoy the moment. A child is a beautiful example of beginner mind. The never ending

questioning of a child who wants to know, so pokes their finger right into the middle of the pile of ripe dog poo. There is newness in every moment causing mothers to cry with exasperation, "How many times do I have to tell you!"

There is innocence in beginner mind. In that lies the deepest protection. Having no expectation requires no protection.

Experience protective instincts

You can still have intentions without expectation. This is the essence of the most powerful energy medicine. How can we know what the best outcome is? If you continuously cling to the fragments of a situation, way of seeing, pattern of behaviour, rather than allowing it to fall away, how can you ever grow? Humans fight terribly hard to remain where they are once they've made up their minds about a thing.

25.2 a) **Dancing With the Wind meditation:** I'm going to guide you through this one, lovely. My voice in your ear. Here are your instructions:

Go to Insight Timer (insighttimer.com/gku) which is a free app. I'm a teacher there. The meditation I want you to listen to is Dancing With the Wind.

Experience 139 Protective Instincts - Meditation

25.2 b) **Journalling:** Write about your wind dancing experience. I'll say nothing else here. Because: spoilers, lovely one. Listen to the meditation; it's an opportunity for a powerful shift.

_____
_____
_____
_____
_____
_____
_____
_____

Chapter 25 Quickening

Experience 140 Protective Instincts - Journalling

26

INVITING CURIOSITY

26.1 The Past in Your Present

I touched on beginner mind and curiosity in the last section. Let's take that further now.

It's exhausting to resist what is real. Reality cannot be defeated; it is. You will always lose a battle with reality. This section is an invitation to explore why you go into battle so often, and so vehemently. And for situations that drain the life out of you, fill you with grief, keep you anxious.

I wonder if chronic fatigue is actually battle fatigue. Food for thought…

I've spent the last five years buried in guilt, its stickiness thick and dense. Resisting reality coated me in the blackest tar of shame. Shame is an elusive blockage.

We never want to cosy up to shame, discover why it's stayed with us for years, or decades, or lifetimes. Which is interesting, since the way to heal shame is to love it without condition. Forgiveness is deep healing and is only a complete spell when it is cast by you, for you.

Nobody else can mix this magic on your behalf, and curiosity is your way in.

Getting curious, and remaining curious, is the beginning of us being the observer of our lives. By observing only, memories of situations, reactions, over-reactions, regrets, victories freely come and go through our observed mind. The gut responses that block any rationality, and underpin the reasons you do everything you do, become another experience to observe. From the position of witness, you can gain understanding of all the perspectives to a situation.

You lose the need to be right. Long-held beliefs are exploded when you become curious about the other's point of view without judging their motivations.

Understanding and compassion creep into the mix and pave the way for forgiveness.

Your mind is brilliant at taking your memories, and replaying them in ways that shake you up. Your armour, never fully packed away, let alone discarded, clangs around your fragile self to protect you from the Big Bad of your memories. The thing is: your memories are often skewed. So often that I'd venture to say that all your memories are figments of your imagination, as are mine.

Few humans have the ability of accurate eidetic recall, especially when they are intimately invested in the outcome. And more especially when the outcome they invested in is what they have built their current existence upon.

Question those pivotal happenings from your past and you risk everything falling apart. What a relief. We are getting to the necessary destruction, the earth-shakers, and the space-makers. This is the thunder of a tiny seed sending its fragile green shoot through the dark earth, into the light.

Experience the past in your present

You're going to do some emotional time travelling. Let's find out where your past appears in your present, and whether you're ready to be kind to yourself. If that sounds a little bit terrifying, buckle up! And remember, take responsibility for your healing, darling. If you need someone to sit with you and hold the space while you do these exercises, go ahead. Call on that handmaid, that trusted person.

Being responsible for taking the steps on the journey doesn't mean you always have to walk alone.

26.1 a) **Journalling:** Write about what is bothering you. What stops you from achieving the success you desire? What memory plays on your mind, proving that you aren't good enough? If you're like me, there will be more than one thing. Make a list. You can do this set of exercises as often as you want.

_____

_____

_____

_____

_____

Chapter 26 — Inviting Curiosity

Experience 141 The Past in Your Present - Journalling

26.1 b) **Visualisation:** Take one of the things you journalled about and put yourself back into that time and place.

When you feel connected, imagine me standing behind you.

I gently put my hand on your shoulder and pull your spirit out of your body, so we are standing together observing you in the situation.

Then you feel a tug on your shoulder again. You find yourself standing behind me and your spirit self, watching us watching you in the situation. This third self is universal mind with infinite compassion and understanding.

In the position of universal mind, float up above the situation to observe the entire scene.

One at a time, take the position of each player in the situation being observed. You are universal mind, able to experience this situation from all perspectives and points of view.

Let the awareness flow through you, universal mind doesn't decide one way or the other, is not a judge. Universal mind is the ultimate witness of your life. Be that now.

When you are finished, float back to stand behind me and spirit you. Walk forward to merge with your spirit body. I gently place my hand on your shoulder and guide your spirit body to merge with your physical body.

Sit in contemplation for a while. Add your new insights to build on your previous journalling entry.

_____

_____

_____

_____

_____

_____

_____

Chapter 26 — Inviting Curiosity

_____
_____
_____
_____
_____
_____
_____
_____
_____
_____
_____

Experience 142 The Past in Your Present - Visualisation

26.1 c) **Moving meditation:** Put on your walking shoes. Go to your favourite walking trail. Imagine this path is your emotional timeline.

Start walking and, every time one of the things you journalled about pops into your mind, stop. Stop right where you are, stay with the memory.

At the side of the path, poke your finger into the earth. Drill a hole, and drop this memory into the hole like a seed.

Gently smooth the surface over the top of your planted seed. You've loosened the earth and made it easier for the new shoot to find the light, to find the surface.

Walk as long as you need to. This is you giving permission for your memories to transform. This is you giving yourself the same permission.

Experience 143 The Past in Your Present - Moving Meditation

26.2 Questions, Curiosity, and Grace

It's hard to stay open to opportunity when we feel unsafe. Insecurity based on wounding past experience stands in the place of a friendly guiding voice, and suspicion rather than curiosity takes over.

"What do they want from me?"

"When are they going to spin around and show me their true faces?"

Asking questions and inviting the unknown is what opens a situation up for growth, but not these kinds of questions. These aren't actually questions, they're accusations. False accusations!

Questions like these have one purpose: to create distance between you and possibility. They keep you packed tight inside your pot. You aren't even root-bound yet, the dirt is hard and moisture can't penetrate to your heart. So a seed you remain.

It's going to get messy before you strike anything resembling glory or Grace though. Muck is the rich basis of the most astonishing growth. My partner is the gardener of plants; I'm the gardener of interior landscapes. In there, on the inside, my thumb is so green it glows emerald. Want to know why? It's because I'm great at sitting on the lawn and watching. I pay attention, offer suggestions. I'm brilliant at suggesting options.

Know what else I'm good at? Smashing pots. I'll teach you how.

Smashing your pot doesn't need to be a violent experience. We shy away from change because it feels dangerous. Of course it does! Danger is thrilling. The thing is you're mixing up your feelings.

Exciting feels the same as dangerous, you just have to consider that the possibility on the other side of change is a good thing. Once you begin to consider, you can get curious about why it's a good thing. Be purposeful in your contemplations, and open to a universe that is on your side.

Thorough and lasting demolition is always going to come from the inside out. You can go through life cradling your pot in your arms like a fragile piece of art, something only to be set on the mantle and admired. Because, look how polished and pretty!

You can walk until exhausted, give up, and hurl your pot against the nearest convenient annoyance for the release of frustration. There! You showed them.

Or, you can water your damn seed. Water it until the pot bursts because you have expanded your concept of yourself. You have grown. Drown yourself in kindness and possibility, let the pot explode and cover you in the muck. Release your heart, that tiny seed that can no longer be bound.

Outside in breaking feels threatening. Inside out breaking feels freeing. You'll know the difference.

Experience questions, curiosity, and grace

I want you to be extra kind to yourself for this experience. It's hard to willingly step into possibility when you've been hurt. All those memories rise up and crowd around you, a protective shield that obscures your view. Let's just get messy and play. It's okay to be messy and imperfect. Everyone is.

26.2 a) **Playing:** Sprout some seeds on cotton wool on your windowsill.

>**Experience 144 Questions, Curiosity, and Grace - Playing**

26.2 b) **Playing:** Make mud pies. If you can get some kids to join in, even better!

>**Experience 145 Questions, Curiosity, and Grace - Playing**

26.2 c) **Playing:** Make mud, fill up some water balloons with the mud, burst those suckers.

>**Experience 146 Questions, Curiosity, and Grace - Playing**

27

EMOTIONAL SHAPE CHANGING

27.1 Your Animal Nature

Shape changing doesn't happen the way supernatural television shows and urban fantasy novels would have you believe. It's an entirely internal process rooted in sensation. Well, I say entirely internal, but that's not strictly accurate.

I get a decidedly wolfish demeanour after working some of my wild magic. My stance steadies, my ability to act decisively kicks up a notch.

My partner's blue eyes glow golden after she's been soaring in a warm air current with a buzzard, and her profile becomes distinctly fierce, her gaze sharper. In those first moments after she returns to earth, she seems much larger than her tiny human frame.

There is a magical menagerie living inside your body. It populates vast plains, and hidden groves. It swims in deep oceans and circles craggy mountain peaks. All of this is inside you.

You can take a breath, side step, and be right there.

Your emotional shape changing takes the forms of many animals. Makes sense, doesn't it? You feel many emotions. In fact, each emotion has subtleties that skew the sensations, so it's not exactly the same feeling each time, even though our limited vocabulary says it's anger, or sadness, or happiness, or whatever.

Experience your animal nature

I'm asking you to touch the edges of what this kind of shape-shifting feels like. You'll get to know a new aspect of yourself and play with your animal nature. You

Part V ⟡ UNFURL

are already an animal—a human animal. Let's take this exploration into wilder realms, away from your domestication, and towards fur, feather, and scale.

27.1 a) **Connecting:** Settle in, do some calming breathing, and tune in to your emotions.

What's going on in your emotional body, right now? There will be one emotion that feels more present than the others.

Where in your body do you feel it?

Give your emotion a colour, size, shape, and texture.

Direct your breath into that part of your body. Let your awareness pour into the emotion there. No judgement, no expectation, just be present with your emotion. Stay here for as long as you need.

You might choose to do only this exercise the first time you try this practice. I support that choice. Get to know your emotional body.

Chapter 27 Emotional Shape Changing

Experience 147 Your Animal Nature - Connecting

27.1 b) **Deepening:** Ask the emotion you are tuned into what animal it wants to be. Have a conversation with your emotion as though it were another being sitting in the room with you.

You don't have to use any formulaic language. Just talk in your own words, with your own understanding and curiosity.

If it feels overwhelming, imagine yourself standing behind the scene, observing your physical self and emotional self in conversation. Be a loving eavesdropper.

Once the conversation has run its course, if you need to reconnect with your physical body, step back into yourself. Breathe down through the soles of your feet and into the earth to ground.

What emotional animal has returned with you?

If you are ready to practise shape-shifting, go on to the next exercise. You might need to take yourself through these visualisations a few times before you feel ready, that's okay. You are the boss of you.

_____
_____
_____
_____
_____
_____
_____
_____
_____
_____
_____
_____

Chapter 27 — Emotional Shape Changing

Experience 148 Your Animal Nature - Deepening

Part V 🜚 UNFURL

27.1 c) **Embodying:** Just as you did in the previous exercise, have a conversation with the animal representation of the emotion upon which you are focused.

You've just met each other. Have that getting-to-know-you conversation. You wouldn't jump someone's bones right after your initial nod of introduction, would you? This might be an exercise that you have to come back to a few times. Take your time! Ask all the questions, you can be as intimate as you dare. I hope you dare.

Eventually, you will reach a point in the conversation (whether it happens the first time you meet, or the seventh) that calls for more than words. You'll know that it's time to go deeper. Your emotional animal will invite you in.

Lean towards them and press your foreheads together. Your bodies are no barrier, and you will merge. What happens next is up to you. Run! Fly! Slither, or crawl. Get wild!

When you are done, come back to your body, which will be right here, safe, awaiting your return.

_____
_____
_____
_____
_____
_____
_____
_____
_____
_____
_____
_____

Experience 149 Your Animal Nature - Embodying

27.2 Shadow Self

The power of earth lends itself to grounding and deep strength. It can also tip into the shadow of bloody-minded stubbornness. Everything, everyone, has a shadow side, shadow self. It's what gives us dimension and forms our fullness.

I watched a lunar eclipse this past weekend. The moon was captivated in the shadow of Mars. She was painted red by degrees and it was a beautiful spectacle. We watched the progress of the shadow through binoculars and were stunned by the difference the presence of the shadow created. The moon was an orb! She was a ball of tangibility, floating just out of reach, not simply a white disc shining in the dark.

The presence of shadow brought her to life and animated the scene. When we are aware of our shadow self, when we are in communication with the dark, when we welcome its presence, it need not be a wounding experience. On the contrary! It is by entering into our shadow space willingly that we claim the power of the experience. Resistance is an energy drain. You will exhaust yourself and, in the end, be claimed by the shadow anyway.

Part V ⟨ornament⟩ UNFURL

I have a way of looking at shadow happenings and drawing from them the healing magic. It shines so clearly even though, to the uninitiated, the scene may appear unrelieved black. They are only looking at the surface of the occurrence, looking and not yet seeing. But one must first be willing to look in order to see.

This is the first step in welcoming our shadow: willingness to engage with the process. It is by softening into the fear and the premonition of imminent devastation that shadow permeates the hard edges of our certainty. Certainty will slice us up, every single time. It's never the shadow that makes us bleed, it's our unwillingness to relinquish our determination to be right to the softness of the shadow.

Being stubborn is not the same as holding boundaries. A boundary is a flexible form, it is supposed to shift and change as you grow. Your boundaries should never restrict your movement, or emotional and spiritual expansion.

Don't be scared to re-evaluate your boundaries. That's the root cause of much of our adult wounding. We are terrified to release the boundary that we set in place when we were eight years old: to never again have to experience that hurtful thing, that unwelcome touch, that unfair comment.

We are so terrified, we do things that maintain the wound, so it continues to scab over and layer new scar tissue over that, decades old.

Experience shadow self

Let's do some gentle shadow work. This experience is not about you taking a deep dive into the darkness. Think of this as taking a rest within the shades you cast.

27.2 a)   **Journalling:** What makes you dig your heels in and resist? It won't take long; in fact, you've already answered the question in your mind. You might have received the answer and quickly disregarded it, but make no mistake—that is the answer.

Begin your journalling session with this internal dialogue. Then write the original prompt: "What makes you dig your heels in and resist?" Transform it into a series of questions you could ask yourself.

For example:

"Why do I refuse to see what's right in front of my nose?"

"Why am I so scared to even look at this?"

"This is stupid, I'm stupid, everything's fine."

Chapter 27 — Emotional Shape Changing

Write out all the questions that come to mind. No censoring! Then, answer them. This is an example of interviewing the Goddess. You have all the answers, you are wiser than you imagine. Don't try to be profound or sound wise. There is no need to be anything other than you. Just have a conversation using your own language. You are enough.

Experience 150 Shadow Self - Journalling

27.2 b) **Moving meditation:** Go outside and observe the shadows being cast by the trees. Watch the way they move, or how they remain still.

Approach the one that calls to you. As you make your way towards it, observe your own shadow.

I want you to get your shadow as close as possible to the tree's shadow without letting them touch.

Pour your awareness into your shadow as you navigate the edges of the tree's shade.

It's fascinating to experience this exercise with the same tree in the day time, and on a moonlit night. You'll embody markedly different sensations, because the magical influences are complimentary. I hope you try it both ways.

_____

_____
_____
_____
_____
_____
_____
_____
_____
_____
_____
_____
_____
_____
_____
_____

Experience 151 Shadow Self - Moving Meditation

Chapter 27 — Emotional Shape Changing

27.2 c) **Shape-shifting:** Begin by placing an anchor outside the shadows you will be working with. This anchor might be an object with which you like to work ritual: it could simply be your cardigan, or your shoes. Bare feet are best for this kind of work, so you could make stepping out of your shoes part of your spellwork. Know this physical thing tethers you to return easily when it's time to come back. You can't get lost. You are safe.

Now, begin with the moving meditation described above in 27.2 b).

You'll know you are ready to shape-shift once you're completely embodying (being embodied by) your shadow.

Merge the edge of your shadow with that of the tree. Slide into the shade, become part of the canopy. You are the tree's shade, and it is yours.

Stay as long as you like. Return when it's time. Trust yourself.

_____
_____
_____
_____
_____
_____
_____
_____
_____
_____
_____
_____
_____
_____
_____

Experience 152 Shadow Self - Shape-shifting

GOING DEEPER

AN INVITATION

*"Had I not created my whole world,
I would certainly have died in other people's."*
—Anaïs Nin

YOUR INVITATION

As you've worked through this guide, your experience of a seed coming to fruit has reached the point in the cycle of unfurling new leaves in the light. You've cast a shadow and are beginning to know shadow's softness, perhaps meeting it properly for the first time.

I hope there are loose pieces of paper stuffed into spaces where you wanted more room to write. I hope there are bits of leaf and twig caught in the pages. I daydream about splashes of mud and juice puckering the pages of your book of wisdom.

I wonder if you understand now how powerful you are. You are the creator of your whole experience, and it's only appropriate I leave you with the first words of this book, bringing you back to the beginning:

> *"Had I not created my whole world, I would certainly have died in other people's."*

I have a collection of guided meditations on Insight Timer; they are free to listen to (insighttimer.com/gku). Come and slip softly into the shadow stuff. I'll hold you in safe space while you explore the sacred nature of your meditative self.

You will discover your internal landscape. Your breath will become a trusted partner in relaxation.

Join me and be nurtured. Plunge new roots deep into the dirt, and shimmy into the power of growing bark.

INDEX OF EXPERIENCE

Active meditation, 156, 161
Anaïs Nin, xi, 1, 43, 45, 71, 73, 111, 113, 165, 167, 219
Breathing, 1, 45, 46, 50, 73, 78, 79, 113, 167
chant, 120
Chanting, 68, 85, 87, 123
Cleansing, 179
Connecting, 7, 8, 20, 29, 30, 34, 38, 140, 141, 208, 209
Contemplation, xvii, 8, 9, 10, 18, 19, 20, 27, 35, 51, 59, 60, 61, 62, 74, 114, 128, 129, 136, 138, 156, 167, 169, 173, 174
Creating space, 14
Creation, 63
Deepening, 3, 4, 15, 17, 31, 33, 38, 41, 54, 75, 99, 152, 163, 164, 174, 175, 182, 183, 188, 189, 194, 195, 210, 211
Divination, 37
Embodying, 1, xi, 104, 108, 121, 129, 212, 213, 221
Energy work, 80, 82
Exploring, 6
Focusing, 30, 31, 38
Grounding, 37, 95, 96
Healing, 1, 92, 93
Invocation, 68, 69
Journalling, 10, 11, 14, 15, 21, 22, 26, 27, 35, 36, 40, 41, 42, 46, 47, 52, 53, 58, 59, 63, 74, 75, 76, 88, 89, 93, 94, 106, 107, 108, 110, 115, 132, 134, 136, 137, 145, 147, 152, 153, 156, 158, 162, 163, 172, 173, 177, 178, 183, 185, 186, 187, 192, 193, 196, 197, 200, 201, 214, 215
Lightening, 51, 55
Listening, 90, 92, 93, 94, 102, 103, 105, 106
Making magic, 169
Meditation, 2, 3, 12, 24, 41, 46, 50, 51, 79, 91, 92, 96, 97, 119, 125, 126, 136, 156, 162, 196, 204, 216
Mindfulness, 23, 56
Moving meditation, 118, 135, 204, 216
Playing, 21, 75, 87, 88, 116, 130, 148, 149, 206
Potion, 66
Relaxation, 40, 124, 125
Release, 139, 154, 178, 179, 205
Remedy, 67
Ritual, 29, 30, 31, 33, 169, 170, 187
Self-inquiry, 59, 60
Sensing, 95, 96, 97, 182, 221
Shape-shifting, 5, 120, 121, 217
Spellwork, 188
Trusting, 6, 7, 57, 132
Visualisation, 29, 79, 80, 84, 85, 98, 119, 120, 144, 145, 150, 151, 202, 203

ABOUT THE AUTHOR

Sondra Turnbull is a holistic therapist and teacher who specialises in helping you let go when you're sure you'll scream and throw a chair through the window the next time someone tells you to let it go.

She's an Aussie living in the Netherlands with her wife, and when she isn't writing, she's creating watercolour and ink artworks or crocheting something tricky, or tweaking recipes to be gluten-free.

Her guided meditations are journeys into deep relaxation and personal wisdom; you can find them on Insight Timer. (Just google it, it's a free app—go nuts!)

She writes richly sensual magical realism novels with lesbian characters, and often explores the mother-daughter dynamic. Always she explores self-love.

Sondra was born in 1972, in Central Queensland, the oldest of five siblings. She moved to Brisbane in her early teens and lived there until her fortieth birthday, when she dared to crack wide open and adventure to the other side of the world, settling in the Netherlands

Subscribe to Sondra's mailing list at
tinyurl.com/GKUloveletters

BOOKS IN THIS SERIES

Embodying Earth: Experiential Guide

The Embodying Earth Experiential Guide includes all guidance contained in this workbook without the ruled lines and extra scribbling space.

Embodying Earth: Personal Journal

The Embodying Earth Journal contains inspirational quotes from the experiential guide, and enough space to pour yourself onto the pages, every day for a year. Use it to record your magical moments and meditative journeys. It is the perfect partner volume for the experiential guide.

Embodying Earth: Personal Workbook

The Embodying Earth Workbook includes everything contained in the experiential guide and also provides space for you to journal, draw, doodle, and scribble. It is your own book of shadows.

GODDESS KINDLED UNIVERSE

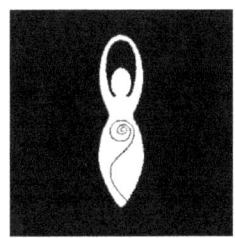

OUR PROMISE

*We are dedicated to showing
you how powerful you are*

*You are not broken.
Let us guide you to remember.
Allow us to hold you safe while you heal.
You are more powerful than you think you are.
Join us, and meet yourself.*